Michel Mazor

The Vanished City

Translated by

David Jacobson

Marsilio Publishers
New York

CONTENTS

THE VANISHED CITY

FOREWORD

In keeping with its program, the Center for Contemporary Jewish Documentation [CCJD, *Centre de Documentation Juive Contemporaine*] publishes texts that may serve in some way as source material for future historians of the tragedy of the Jews under the Swastika.

Most of our prior publications have been based on documents from the camp of the oppressor—enabling us to reconstruct, part by part, the terrifying machinery of extermination. Only once before the present volume have we published an account by a victim of racist barbarism. I am thinking of Georges Wellers's moving *De Drancy à Auschwitz,* which made such a deep, vast impact through its author's human qualities and its rigorous objectivity.

In Michel Mazor's *La Cité engloutie* [The Vanished City], the oppressor does not, so to speak, appear on the scene—only his criminal intent is everywhere present. What this book shows us are the reactions within a community of hunted victims, the way of life that community adopts, and the state of mind that prevails in it. Let me add that this book is unique in imparting this to us, for the whole story is told by one of the very few survivors of the tragedy of the Warsaw ghetto, and one endowed with keen psychological insight, a gift for observation, an intellectual honesty, and an objectivity the reader will no doubt appreciate.

3

I think that to grasp the spirit in which Michel Mazor deals with his subject, it is useful to know something of his antecedents. His father was a prominent lawyer in Kiev, a professor of civil law, as well as one of the pioneers of the burgeoning Zionist movement. The noblest traditions of the Russian Jewish intelligentsia guided this family—which is to say that the interest it took in social issues in general and Jewish issues in particular was lively and passionate. Having himself become a lawyer, Michel Mazor left his native Russia during the Civil War to settle in Poland. He joined the bar in Warsaw, the Polish capital that was also home to what was then the largest Jewish community in Europe. Well before the Second World War the younger Mazor took part in the activities of various Jewish social organizations.

After the outbreak of the war, the defeat of Poland, and the Nazi occupation, Mazor, like all his Jewish fellow citizens, found himself confined to the famous Warsaw ghetto, hallowed in memory as both tragic and inspiring. There he devoted himself to social activity, which brought him a thorough knowledge of the inner structure of that strange society, sealed off in a narrow site and engulfed in the end by the floodtides of Hitler's barbarism—after the sublime leap to action of April 1943.

Mazor's illumination—a first in the historical literature of the Second World War—of psychological aspects of the ghetto's inner life lends his testimony a very special interest. A perceptive and objective observer, he notes the quiet, humble courage, the deep sense of solidarity, and the human compassion, as well as the negative sides of the ghetto's social life.

Mazor was not to experience the bloody hours of revolt: deported and bound for the extermination camp of Treblinka at the end of 1942, he owed his salvation only to his escape from a cattle car.

Much of his testimony was published in installments in our magazine *Le Mond Juif,* and immediately aroused enormous interest both among specialists and the public at large. The major historical publications that have appeared since cite Mazor's text and pay tribute to its author. In discussing the persecution of the Jews in his book *La Solution finale* [The Final Solution] Gérald Reitlinger refers several times to *La Cité engloutie,* which he describes as "a survey of the ghetto's social problems, treated with startling sobriety." He characterizes Michel Mazor as "the most impartial witness."

The historian Philip Friedman quotes numerous passages from the book, which he defines as "a detailed, conscientious, and well-founded study of the life and hardships of the ghetto, written by a survivor."

The disappearance of the Jewish community of Warsaw, that incomparable center of Jewish culture, was one of Judaism's most painful losses. Its consequences are incalculable. For this reason the CCJD considered it its duty to devote one of its first publications to the glorious revolt of the Warsaw ghetto as seen from the point of view of one of the hangmen, in this case the sinister Stroop; now we are pleased to publish an extremely valuable testimony of the inner life of this community during the last years of its existence and thus to pay a final homage to it from the bottoms of our wounded hearts.

I. Schneersohn,
President of the CCJD

TO THE READER

The Vanished City *is neither a monograph nor a history of the Warsaw ghetto, but rather my personal recollections of life there. It is not my intention, however, to speak of myself, but to convey the state of mind of the people forced to undergo the great ordeal that was the ghetto. My goal is less to recount its horrors (which are well known) than to present the observations I made of myself and those close to me, to show our attitude toward the events of those desperate years, to recreate the moral climate of the ghetto—that indescribable state of feverish hopelessness coupled, despite everything, with a faith in liberation, "the deep optimism," as André Gide writes, "that always attends the martyred."*

For a long time I fought the temptation to write my memoirs. It is too painful to focus one's mind on the events of terrible years, to rouse the ghosts of departed friends, or if only in one's mind, to ply those obliterated streets.

If I have nevertheless written these recollections, I owe the fact to the insistence of two long-time friends, Mr. I. Schneersohn, the President of the Center of Contemporary Jewish Documentation, and Mr. I. Machover, President of the Federation of Jewish Relief Organisations of Great Britain, whose authority managed to overcome my inner resistance. In publishing my book I eagerly extend to both my sincere gratitude.

I. GENERAL REMARKS ON THE GHETTO

Before the recent war, the word "ghetto" evoked for us something quite remote in space as well as time: it was common knowledge that in North Africa, among populations not very advanced culturally, the Jews still lived in quarters reserved especially for them; that at one time, in the Middle Ages, ghettos existed in Western Europe; and that tourists would visit the traces of Germany's ghettos much as they would its feudal castles.

For contemporary man the very notion of a ghetto seems linked to a past long since vanished. In the era immediately preceding the Second World War, when the rising tide of totalitarian ideology—and not only in Germany—swept a revived anti-semitism into its muddy waters, into an atmosphere charged with vague but fearsome threats, the gloomy forebodings gave rise to certain literary works predicting imminent catastrophe for Jewry. Thus I can recall reading around this time an English short story depicting the imaginary wanderings of exiled European Jews through the Gobi Desert, their designated resettlement site.

In Poland a novel appeared about the transfer of the Jews to Madagascar (an idea that was taken seriously and was even fairly popular in Polish circles). According to this novel, only 100,000 privileged Jews were to remain in Poland after the exile.

But the authors of these pessimistic utopias never ventured to imagine that in contemporary Europe the walls of ghettos could be erected again. Unfortunately, reality far surpassed their imagination: the ghettos really returned in Europe and, worse, were mere stops on a route that, alas, was to lead much further than Madagascar.

Those who reinstated the ghettos, the Nazis themselves, feared the impression this reconstruction might create; and with their characteristic mixture of primitive brutality and shrewd treachery, they hoped to mislead world opinion by forbidding the use of the term "ghetto," which they replaced with the more harmless-sounding one of "Jewish quarter" (*Judenviertel*)—nor, incidentally, did such ruses always fail to achieve the intended effect.

The most important of these Jewish quarters was that of Warsaw. This ghetto housed not only the most populous Jewish community in Europe, that of the Polish capital, but also the Jewish masses that had fled there from other Polish cities annexed by the Third Reich (Lodz, etc.). Moreover, for the entire duration of the Warsaw ghetto, the Germans kept adding to it Jewish populations expelled from nearby cities and small towns. It is likely that at one point the ghetto population rose to 400,000 or more (though no precise figure exists).

Founded in October 1940, and completely razed in April 1943, this mirage-city disappeared almost without a trace.

It strikes me that never before in history—not even in the most terrible and catastrophic epochs—has any generation on the face of the earth amassed a spiritual experience comparable to that which the handful of survivors of the Warsaw ghetto carry within them. Everything around them disappeared—the milieu in which they had lived, their relatives, their friends, ordinary acquaintances, the people they kept company with for many years as well as those they knew only by sight or encountered through public or private dealings. Many families completely disappeared, without leaving behind even distant relatives as survivors, or so much as a family photo, or a single identifiable tomb . . . . Spiritual values and immense creative forces perished with those who were to keep their memory alive. Of the city itself nothing survives but apocalyptic ruins.

The number of documentary materials required for studying the history of the Warsaw ghetto is plainly insufficient. The archives of Doctor Ringelblum—had they survived in their entirety—would have been able in part to fill this gap. This Jewish historian, who tragically disappeared, realized from the very first day of the catastrophe how important it would be to have preserved a faithful record of our improbable epoch. At the same time, he was one of the most active and dedicated community workers (an aspect of his activity to which I shall return in the text that follows). Often I had occasion to exchange views with him about the archives he was assembling: his goal was to preserve documentary testimony not only of the persecutions and sufferings, but also of the internal evolution of Jewish life, the work of social organizations, and the activity of the authorities. To the best of my knowledge, no one has yet managed to rediscover Ringelblum's archives in their entirety; as valuable as the parts recovered are, they are still not sufficient to allow an in-depth study of all aspects of life in the Warsaw ghetto.

Another source of information are the testimonies of survivors. On the one hand, however, such witnesses are few, and on the other hand, the complexity and uniqueness of ghetto life were such that no individual experience could ever encompass all its aspects. Furthermore, in focusing on only particular aspects and leaving out others, such first-hand testimonies risk distorting the perspective needed for an exact analysis of facts.

As for me, I was involved—even before the creation of the ghetto, from the years 1939–40—in the formation of Tenement Committees in the Public Sector of Mutual Aid. The question of the role of these Tenement Committees in ghetto life will figure prominently in the following narrative: for now, let me simply explain that in my duties as president of the Commission of Instruction and Inspection of Tenement Committees for the Sixth District (the poorest and most solidly working-class in the city) and as president of the Central Commission of Tenement Committees, I had frequent contact with the population, both through the public assemblies, and through daily encounters with hundreds of people: representatives of the various Tenement Committees and aides who kept me abreast of the situation within these organizations. In these meetings I also spoke with representatives of the different social organizations and political parties. All these contacts opened up a vast field of observation for me, enabling me to follow the fluctuations in mood and outlook of the masses, the general trend of social and living conditions in the ghetto, as well as the work of social organizations.

Even more than their insufficiency it is their partiality that requires survivors' testimonies to be used for historical purposes only with great caution—for, whether conscious or not, such partiality does lead to factual distortion. This distortion comes, for instance, from exaggerating the role the narrator's favored "side" played in events.

Be that as it may, we are forced to acknowledge that we

possess too little material to undertake a rigorous study of the Warsaw ghetto: in my opinion neither a sociology nor an economy of the ghetto can ever be written.

Such works will be utterly impossible for future generations. Even today my personal experience teaches me that the most one can attempt is to establish a sort of phenomenology of the ghetto; in other words, a general description of features, unique in their concrete density, specific to the life of this incredible society.

Stefan Zweig remarks in his memoirs (*The World of Yesterday*) "that it is infinitely easier to reconstruct the facts of an epoch than its moral climate." In the case of the ghetto, this difficulty of reconstituting the genuine atmosphere of the past becomes a total impossibility: no recourse to analogies or comparisons is permitted, for the horror and pathos of the ghetto remain absolutely exceptional, unique, unprecedented; ordinary human language cannot possibly provide an adequate description of the life and destiny of the ghetto. And without this, no accumulation of details, no matter how abundant, could ever acquire real value from a historical perspective. Here I see only a major, insurmountable difficulty.

To attempt to imagine the ghetto's moral climate, the contemporary reader would first have to make a twofold effort. First, he would have to transport himself mentally to the years 1940–42, all the while barring from consciousness his knowledge of the fate that ultimately befell the ghetto. For, in light of its horrific end, any characteristic feature of the life of this ephemeral site risks seeming insignificant: should one praise or blame, exalt or curse phenomena one knows are doomed to soon disappear? The people hemmed into the ghetto, however, did not know the fate awaiting them (at least until 1942); indeed the majority of them knew nothing of that fate till death suddenly struck. They lived the life imposed upon them without knowing any other; which is why the struggle and sufferings, the acts of heroism and the weakness of the people of the ghetto lose none of their human and historic interest through what the contemporary reader might view as the brevity of their saga.

How was the Warsaw ghetto created? In October of 1940, the Jewish inhabitants of the city were installed there by the hundreds of thousands: men and women, young and old; world-renowned scholars as well as illiterates, idealists as well as profiteers, freethinkers and the Orthodox; the result was a motley society possessing all the boundless differences that make up any large environment. All its human groupings were forced into close cohabitation. Everyone was housed in already overcrowded apartments, overlooking narrow streets, doubly closed-up in this site surrounded by walls. The sealing off of the ghetto was decreed on November 15, 1940; later, a special edict threatened anyone attempting to break out with capital punishment—nor was this an idle threat. The situation of those thrust into the ghetto after its formation was particularly tragic: these hapless people, expelled from cities and small towns surrounding the capital, came with no more than hand luggage, which was often stolen from them on their arrival; they were obliged to make do with accommodations known as "Refugee Centers."

From the outset, the ghetto was overpopulated; furthermore, its area continually shrank as blocks of apartment houses and even whole streets were gradually removed from it: the inhabitants of those streets would then swell the ranks, already well beyond capacity, of those in the reduced ghetto; squeezing the refugees in became an almost insurmountably hard problem. Unsolvable in life, the problem was resolved by death: the mortality rate in the refugee centers was so high that there was a constant turnover in population, new arrivals replacing the dead—though again rather briefly. Often such centers lacked even the most basic hygiene; they forced people to live on top of one another in the most unspeakably degrading disorder—men forced to cohabit with women, young with old, the hale with the sick. Hunger and lice—the carriers of typhus—were the true masters of the house.

The hospital for typhoid victims was likewise crammed beyond capacity and the sick tried everything not to be taken there. Since every typhus sufferer had to be reported and isolated, families would camouflage their sick, who, with fevers of 104°F, would make superhuman efforts to stay on their feet and allay suspicion. By remaining among the healthy, of course, they further spread the disease.

I recall seeing some twenty refugees arrive one day at a center, after they had been expelled from Vilanov, a small city outside of Warsaw (I believe it was in the autumn of 1941). These people had certainly not had an easy time of it that year; yet they had been able to remain in their own homes, and to walk in the fields, and their skin was still tan from the sun. Among the group was a young woman who smiled as she talked with a man who held her hand . . . .

How can I explain what I felt, watching these men and women arrive still healthy and normal, unsuspecting of the fate that awaited them? They had no inkling that in a very short time, hunger, filth, deprivation, sickness, and a promiscuous lack of privacy would transform them into living corpses—emaciated or inordinately swollen—with only agony and death to follow. A terrible fatality hung over these people, and nothing in the life of the ghetto could deflect its implacable course.

I cannot cite by memory the total numbers of inhabitants of the refugee centers during the various phases of their existence. What is indisputable, however, is that at the moment the *Große Aktion* [Great Action] started there were far fewer people in the Centers than at the start.

In the period in question the Centers held only six or seven thousand refugees—the unfortunates who were to make up the first deportation convoys. On July 22, 1942, all Center inhabitants were led off for the horrible camp of Treblinka; and this spelled the end of the Centers. After the roundup that day, I happened to be near one such center: I witnessed the return of two of its residents, who, having been away at the time of the roundup, had not been included in the deportation; when they found out what had happened, they decided to catch up with the convoy. All entreaties were in vain. Their lives had become so burdensome to them, that any change was welcome.

Naturally there was no lack of goodwill on the part of the community welfare workers, and although all efforts seemed doomed to failure, people did their utmost to mitigate the cruel fate of "Center" residents. Among the members of the Tenement Committees, relief committees were organized to assist them; the Tenement Committees themselves were involved with certain centers. I can cite, for example, the one at 12 Elektoralna Street. Its patronage committee included Mme O. Minska (who later disappeared in the ghetto) and my wife; it was financed by the committee from our own apartment building at 32 Elektoralna, one of the wealthiest residences, and further funded by private contributions that the women collected.

The committee of patrons supervised the meals of the Center residents at the kitchen of Mutual Aid; it oversaw deliveries, and made sure the allotted fat content actually made its way into the food (two grams per person); after which, the meal was distributed, accompanied by a round loaf of bread. The committee called upon the services of a physician, who regularly visited the center, monitored its hygiene, and did his utmost to maintain the morale of the residents. Once when a male baby was born, a circumcision reception was organized. Alas! the child did not live more than six weeks, and his father, worn out by his labors in a German workshop, preceded him into death's kingdom.

I have an especially vivid recollection of a *Seder* organized in this Center by the Patronage Committee at Passover 1942. The *Seder* had taken on a very solemn character. The menu had nothing classical about it (a porridge, a soup, vegetables, coffee), but for once everyone could at least eat his fill. The residents greedily cleaned their plates, returning for seconds. The unaccustomed satisfaction put a fevered glow into their faces. After the meal, the administrator of the Center gave a speech. This was a certain Mr. Tsalal from Palestine, who had left the Holy Land in August 1939 with his wife and son, a three-year-old "sabra," to visit relatives in Warsaw, where events had halted their journey. Tsalal's message that night was that we were not alone in the world, that everywhere, in London, in New York, our brethren were thinking of us. Deliverance would come, we had only to hold out until it did!

One would have to have been at this scene to imagine the infinitely tragic notes these optimistic words struck in people now living without a shred of hope in the world.

II. THE ATTITUDE OF THE JEWS
TOWARD PERSECUTIONS AND PERSECUTORS

It takes no great knowledge of Jewish history to note the essential difference between the ghettos of the Middle Ages and those created by the Master Race. The former were not completely cut off from the world: Jews could leave them by day; ordinary life took on forms that allowed generations of Jews to live and to succeed one another upholding their distinctive traditions, even creating a civilization.

The medieval ghettos still represented a form of life—one organized, it is true, at a remove from the world. In the twentieth century, especially in Warsaw, the ghetto was no longer anything but an organized form of death—a "little death chest" (*Todeskästchen*), as it was called by one of the German sentries posted at its gates.

The entry into the ghetto of goods and supplies fell within the jurisdiction of an institution called the *Transferstelle:* the quantities let in were so meager, the rationing of food cards so inadequate, that normally no human being could survive more than a short time in the ghetto. If this was not the case, if the agony of the ghetto was prolonged, it was thanks to the food-smuggling made possible by the corruption the Germans failed to eliminate in their own ranks. Life in the Warsaw ghetto continued despite German regulations. Had these rules ushered in a reign of authentic German-style order, the entire ghetto population would have succumbed to starvation.

In the Warsaw ghetto, the Nazis constructed on the level of concrete reality a world that the renowned Martin Heidegger conceived on a philosophical plane—though, no less, to the glory of his *Führer*. In Heidegger's view, the world exists only as a site of death; man is thrown into the world, has lost his way in it, if not into it; the only way out of it being death—that "being unto death" that is the essence of life.

The ghetto is surely a phenomenon of the "concentrational universe"; but if we consider it as it appeared to the eyes of its creators, we will be better able to account for what distinguished the essential traits of this "universe" from the concentration camps.

The powers that use such camps claim that those interned in them are expiating some crime or misdemeanor, that they spend a certain set period of time in them for the purpose of "reeducation," and that one should give them work while watching over their condition. For the ghetto inhabitant there is no need for such learned camouflage, for play-acting of this sort: the Germans simply crammed people in once and for all, without bothering to accuse them of any fault, without the least concern for their futures.

Whereas the concentration camp represented a meticulously regulated machine, and its inner organization was completely rigid, the ghetto had no internal structure. It was unbridled chaos, into whose whirlwinds victims were randomly tossed. This is why the most helpless among the ghetto inhabitants, those who died right out on the sidewalk, exposing their hunger-swollen legs to passersby, could feel, more than camp inmates could, that they were living at the furthest limits of decay and abandonment in the strange universe surrounding them.

In the shattered, chaotic world of the ghetto, all vital and social movements assumed monstrous forms, as though reflected in a distorting mirror: one need only recall the "state interventionism" of the Lodz ghetto, the "free play of economic forces" put in practice by the *Judenrat* [Jewish Council] of the Warsaw ghetto, and the megalomania of the Jewish authorities in both places.

Not only the very notion of the "concentrational universe," coined by David Rousset,* but also the characteristic features this author traces, are found in the ghetto, which was also a fruit of "Ubu-esque inspiration" and "Kafkaesque obsession."

Yet Kafkaesque man, ever more ensnared in the traps an unfathomable world holds out to him, while making vain efforts to break loose from them, basically knows neither what he wants nor where he is going; he is himself a mere product of this absurd world, and therein lies the cause of his helpless situation.

The mentality of the ghetto, conversely, was characterized by its clearly established finality—the key element in its psychological structure. The ghetto strove to hold out against everything, despite all its horrors and sufferings, to endure for the dawn of earthly deliverance. Even in the face of overwhelming evidence to the contrary, faith in final victory and in the defeat of Nazism was never extinguished in the hearts of most of the ghetto's inhabitants; even in the most horrific periods, every favorable rumor, however fantastic, sufficed to

---

* D. Rousset, *L'Univers concentrationnaire* (1946), translated into English as *The Other Kingdom*, New York, 1947. [Translator's note.]

unleash a wave of optimism which, against a background of boundless despair and suffering, cast a glimmer of hope over the whole ghetto.

It is interesting to note that there were few suicides in the ghetto, or at least not in the period that concerns us. The Germans only despised the Eastern European Jews more for this: the German Jews, "their own" Jews, often enough resorted to suicide in far less dire straits. Clearly, the Germans could not understand that every Jew in the ghetto clung to life in the hope of witnessing the defeat of Nazism, if only for an instant, and to see the dawning of a more just world.

I was able to see further evidence of this state of mind in the following circumstances: around mid-August 1942, at the height of the mass deportations, I was part of the group of some thousand Jews housed in the Landau brothers' small factory on Gesia Street. We slept practically on top of one another, on the floor or on the sawdust; most of us, having come down with dysentery, were suffering from malnutrition. So, we were in quite a precarious situation: the Germans, having exhausted the supply of officially deportable people, had started to raid the factories: in ours, they rounded up nearly all the women and children on one day alone (some three hundred people). This "blockade" grew more and more frequent: with every raid we would be lined up in the courtyard and the SS officer would choose his victims altogether arbitrarily. Thus he once picked all men who were unshaven: as it happened, they were skilled workers. After this roundup, the plant was manned by merchants, lawyers, social workers, etc. Despite everything, we believed at the time that some might manage against all odds to survive in the factory; and we all said to each other: "Let's hope at least one of us survives to tell people what happened here."

Not far from our factory, at one end of the street, there was a residential building that received no protection of any kind. The residents—the "core" residents so to speak—had been deported at the start of the *Aktion,* but the building was continually haunted by people who had ventured out of other parts of the ghetto. Alas! these guests' stays were to be short—at most a few days, sometimes only a few hours; whereupon new shades would edge their way in to take the place of the ones that had disappeared . . .

One day, in the courtyard of our factory, we witnessed the arrival of one such transient guest. He was an upholsterer by profession. While chatting with me, he offered to rent me a cot for five zlotys a night. It was a proposition I gleefully accepted. Two days later he informed me: twenty-five zlotys a week. Such transactions seemed then quite haphazard, since neither party in the deal had much chance of surviving a full week; yet I took the gamble. As we said our goodbyes the upholsterer made the following speech to me: "We're in a time now when you have to live and want to live despite everything. Before, if a person had to give up a nice apartment for a more modest one, or couldn't pay his bills, he'd jump out a window . . . . Today things are different . . . Nothing can force a Jew to take his own life . . . . You want to live to see how things will be after . . . ." Never again did I see my trading partner: I inherited the cot, but not for long, of course, because I myself was deported on September 4, 1942. In his unassuming speech this naive philosopher of the ghetto accurately summed up the specific mental attitude most of the Jews had toward the terrifying reality in which they lived and the inhuman persecutions they were the victims of: "You have to endure at any price; the ghetto is something that's been inflicted on us from without; but we'll overcome all that, the humane order of things can't not revive among men."

On a purely spiritual plane, Judaism repudiated the idea of the ghetto—on a more general plane, Judaism was resolutely pitted against the Germans, and was so from the very start of the occupation. Whatever humiliations the Germans imposed on us came from without, and could not undermine the deep sense we had of our human dignity. Here is a scene that illustrates this stance: shortly before the ghetto came into existence, I was walking along Marszalkowska Street with a friend, both of us wearing our Jewish armbands. Suddenly we found ourselves face to face with two German boys about fifteen or sixteen years old, dressed in the uniform of some Nazi paramilitary organization. The two boys started shouting, and it became clear to us that they were demanding that "the Jews" take off their hats to them. With the utmost seriousness we lifted our caps; we looked at one another: the two Germans were holding riding crops, and it was obvious that they could, if they so desired, whip us with perfect impunity until we bled. Yet we sensed that they suddenly felt helpless and perplexed—as if they had understood in a flash that, for all the blows they might inflict with all the riding crops in the world, they would never penetrate to the source of our human consciousness, they could inflict sufferings on us but not subjugate our spirit . . . . For a moment the boys looked at us, and then, with a gesture of the hand that betrayed their disillusionment, turned on their heels and went off . . . .

The Jews of Warsaw spontaneously adopted this spiritual attitude from the very start of the persecutions. Well before the ghetto, life had been made intolerable for them; people ridiculed them, tormented them in a thousand ways. It was impossible for them to appear on the streets, where they would be subject to incessant roundups and forced to perform labors that were entirely useless and absurd—and often accompanied by beatings. Here are some randomly cited episodes that took place within one brief period: they involved Jewish tenants from the apartment building at 23 Wilcza, which we were living in at the start of the occupation, and a few other tenants from nearby. A Jewish engineer returned home one day with his fur-lined coat turned inside out: the Germans had forced him to make a fool of himself in front of a crowd of jeering passersby. On another occasion, it was a young Jew who came home with his face bloody and disfigured: a Gestapo agent, spotting him on the street with his overcoat over his arm, had claimed he was using the coat to hide his Jewish armband—an alleged misdemeanor he punished on the spot.

On the night between December 31, 1939 and January 1, 1940, the Germans burst into one of the apartments, where a fairly large group was gathered, made up mostly of refugees from Lodz. They forced the young people, men and women, to strip completely, merely to make them view each other in their nakedness.

Another day, I noticed two Germans on the street who were goading ahead of them a young Jewish man in evening dress, complete with tails and top hat. I learned that, in searching his home, the Germans discovered these clothes; outraged, they devised this outlandish punishment.

A young woman, Mira J., told me that, after being rounded up on the street, she was forced to wash the barracks floors using her own silk lingerie as a rag. One could cite an infinite number of such incidents, many of which had far graver outcomes. Life had undoubtedly become hell; yet if our bodies were defenseless, our souls were steeled by torment, made invulnerable to these butchers in their innermost, hidden regions, where we maintained our true dignity. The Germans caused us suffering, but their insults failed to hurt us; they could annihilate us, but not subjugate us. That is why no Jew has felt ashamed to tell what he endured at the hands of the Nazi hangmen. One couldn't consider these tortures as something done to human beings by other human beings; they were more like the bites of a rabid dog, or damage caused by lightning.

One could even go so far as to claim that the Jews did not hate the Germans in the normal meaning of the term: for hate presupposes the presence, even from a very remote perspective, of a sort of community with its object, a community of kind—the differences, the causes for hostility, only take second place. That is how men can hate their fellow human beings. But what was still human about these creatures with their dull-witted, ruthless faces, their fierce, howling voices, beating a bizarre time with their boots?

We felt they were something so different, so alien, that we categorically refused to place them on any plane of human values; the nightmare had settled on the world in totally incomprehensible fashion, but surely in the end would be dispelled if man, the bearer of spiritual values, were to survive.

It was from this spirit of refusal, of a spiritual rejection of concrete reality, that all the positive currents, and all the pathos of the ghetto sprang: the passive resistance engendered by a steadfastness of soul, a contempt for danger that even extended to conscious sacrifice on the part of a great many community workers, and finally a glorious apotheosis, the armed revolt of 1943.

It is common knowledge, however, that no human society is monolithic: the ghetto, too, had its share of people who did not raise themselves up to the spiritual plane we have spoken of, who in fact debased themselves in accepting the facts and trying to make accommodations and compromises.

I remember one encounter I had near the ghetto walls. My interlocutor, a very cultivated engineer, was a man of experience. The conversation began with a recital of the hardships and setbacks the Germans were suffering, news I thought should be spread without placing too much trust in it. The engineer's only reply was: "Give up these fantasies. No one is going to outwit the Germans: we'll be here in the ghetto a long time, maybe as long as fifty years."

At the time, I asked him: "If that's how it is, what keeps you from dashing your skull out against that wall there?"

Yet obviously those who accepted the ghetto had no desire to dash out their brains. They had settled into the ghetto for good and, in order to make their life as comfortable as they could, were not going to put up a fuss about their choice of means.

This spirit, prevalent in certain sectors of the ghetto, was the source of all its negative aspects: the insatiable greed of the big-time smugglers and the owners of workshops using slave labor; the megalomania of the communal administration, which saw itself as a genuine state power; the corruption of its outer circles; the abuses among food suppliers; last but not least, the shameful criminal actions of the Jewish police.

The megalomania of the communal authorities at times bordered on the grotesque. Numerous anecdotal accounts have dealt with them; for never, even in the most horrific days, did the ghetto lose its sense of humor. The president of the *Judenrat,* or Jewish Council, the engineer Adam Czerniakow, lived on Chlodna Street, not far from the bridge built specifically to allow passage from one part of the ghetto to the other. This gave rise to the following explanation: The bridge in question was built so that the president of the *Judenrat* would have no reason to envy the president of the Polish Republic, whose residence was also near a bridge—albeit one over the Vistula.

Likewise it was rumored that, on noting the presence on the ghetto streets of two German soldiers, the *Judenrat* had written a letter to the government of the Reich protesting this violation of its territorial sovereignty (Germans, in fact, were forbidden to enter the ghetto, to avoid possible contagion—*Seuchengefahr*).

Moving from stories to reality, one must concede that the *Judenrat* protected and secured important administrative posts for people completely removed from Judaism; before the war these people had openly flaunted their non-Jewishness and on occasion committed acts harmful to the Jews. To reproaches about this, the president of the *Judenrat* responded: "We are no longer the Israelite community of prewar times, but the Jewish sector of the capital, where all inhabitants enjoy the same rights . . . ."

I learned of this dialogue from someone who took part in the conversation with the president—one of the major figures in Warsaw Jewry, the late, much-missed Sophia Syrkin-Birstein, a physician, and a longtime friend of mine.

It seems, however, that personally president Czerniakow was a man of goodwill, though surrounded by the wrong people. If he did not always live up the difficult role he had to play, he atoned for this by the dignity with which he died. On learning, at the start of the Germans' *Große Aktion* of 1942, that the Nazis expected the *Judenrat* to provide contingents of deportees, he took poison. The community's situation was dire, of course, and no problem in this city of

death that was the Warsaw ghetto could find a positive solution. Yet it cannot be claimed that the Jewish authorities did
all they could to relieve even a little, even temporarily, the
sufferings of the neediest and most helpless among us.

III. *JUDENRÄTE* IN GENERAL
AND
WARSAW'S *JUDENRAT* IN PARTICULAR

The administrations of the Jewish communities (*Judenräte*), named by the Germans, were not essentially organs of Jewish autonomy. They were instruments created by the Germans to help them accomplish their schemes for the Jews, which primarily meant consolidation into the ghetto, divestment, and deportation—with as much of this as possible to be carried out by the Jews themselves.

The facts have shown that it was force of circumstance that led the *Judenräte* to execute the Germans' orders in all these areas. It was foreseeable that this would be their role (though obviously one could not imagine beforehand the heights Hitler's ferocity would reach), and it strikes me that, on becoming a member of the *Judenrat*, every Jew should have realized the role he had been called to play and the responsibility he assumed. There can be no doubt, of course, that some of the members of the *Judenräte* were sincerely convinced that, under existing conditions, the fate of the persecuted Jews could be mitigated only by these institutions. In regulating intra-Jewish relations, this was to some degree true. But that cannot alter the fact that those who became, by the will of the Germans, "Führer Jews," were inevitably obliged, regardless of their good intentions, to fol-

31

low a fatal course that made them pawns in the hands of the enemy.

From time to time I would hear certain members of the *Judenräte* claim that they had been appointed by the Germans without their consent and quite against their will. It is possible that in a very few cases, someone given the post of *Obmann* (president) of the *Judenrat* had in fact been forced to accept it, but the majority of such titleholders were under no such constraint. And furthermore, there was always the possibility of keeping in the background, to avoid being noticed by the Germans. It can generally be stated, then, that people became members of the *Judenrat* by their own choosing; and there was no shortage of candidates. The temptation was only too obvious, for in the first years of occupation, belonging to the *Judenrat* meant a privileged situation both in terms of material well-being and of personal safety. The Germans knew how to reward their personnel, as long as they needed them. No doubt as events unfolded, certain members of the *Judenräte* took a second look at their role, and went through an intense inner struggle, seeking to atone for their errors and shirk the responsibility to carry out fatal orders. We have already mentioned the suicide of the engineer Czerniakow, president of the Warsaw *Judenrat*. I also knew of another case in which the vice-president of the *Judenrat* of the city of Zamosc (if I remember correctly, his name was Szeps) went to the head of a train of deportees and, to encourage his fellow prisoners, boarded the death train with them. Yet all these cases in no way alter the fact that in occupied Poland the *Judenräte* were nothing but a German tool, and were regarded as such by the population under their control. Perhaps in certain provincial towns this situation was slightly alleviated by the fact that there the *Ju-*

denräte showed more good will and flexibility: through corruption of local authorities, they managed somewhat to improve general living conditions. As far as I know, no one in
the provincial ghettos died of hunger—at least that was one
nightmare they were spared.

It was in Warsaw that the true, obvious character of the
Judenrat was revealed, and as such incurred the hatred of the
masses; the overwhelming majority of Tenement Committees adopted a policy of noncollaboration. All efforts of the
Judenrat to gain a hold on these committees and make them
their tools met with fierce resistance. It is significant, to appreciate the mentality of the people, that in my district of
Mutual Aid, the Sixth—the most populous and poorest part
of the city—access to the general meeting of Tenement
Committees was virtually closed, even to the technical officials of the *Judenrat*. I recall that at one meeting held in the
district hall, when it was made known that the speaker who
had taken the floor was a collaborator with the *Judenrat*, the
indignation that mounted against him grew so threatening,
it was all I could do to get him out of the meeting un-
harmed.

The role of the *Judenrat* and of the Jewish police in the *Große
Aktion* of 1942 will be dealt with separately, together with the
question of mass deportations to the extermination camp of
Treblinka. Here, to give an idea of the functions the *Judenrat*
was obliged to fulfill, let me recount the following incident.

At the end of December 1941, the Germans issued an
edict demanding that the Jews of the Warsaw ghetto turn
over all the fur coats and fur clothing in their possession:
pelisses, collars, muffs, down to the most insignificant articles of clothing. There was a sanction added to this edict:

possession by a Jew of the smallest scrap of fur in any form would be grounds for instant execution.

As ever, it was the *Judenrat* that carried out the order. In severe cold, long lines stood before the *Judenrat* warehouses; over his arm each Jew held his warm clothing, which he turned over to the Germans. The order was carried out in exemplary fashion; the Germans even expressed their satisfaction with it to the *Judenrat*.

Furthermore, the *Judenrat* was the mouthpiece for the Germans, even in the case of their most hideous crimes.

Thus, on the night of April 17, 1942, a massacre of highly respected community relief workers took place in the Warsaw ghetto. The following day, by morning, we received news at the Center for Mutual Aid of these nocturnal killings, which were all carried out in the same fashion. A detachment of Germans took the victim from his apartment and shot him at close range with a revolver, leaving the corpse in the street. The killers had come into the ghetto with a list of victims and their addresses. Their mission had been established in advance and was meticulously carried out. In total fifty-two people were assassinated, many of them colleagues of mine in community relief work. Among them was a gifted young statistician, Menachem Linder; also, one of the most active social workers, E. Kagan, organizer of people's kitchens as well as of Tenement Committees and the first president of the Central Commission of those committees; and so many others!

At first sight of the list of those killed, it was hard to know what had determined the choice of victims. This apparently was the first incident of killing off the ranks of social activists. The incident caused great disquiet in the ghetto; many now decided not to risk sleeping in their own homes.

Two or three days later, there appeared a communiqué from the *Judenrat* announcing that the *Aktion* was over, and that the victims had been punished for "taking an interest in matters that did not concern them."

The communiqué was rather ambiguous: on the one hand, it was reassuring—for the moment new killings were not on the horizon; but on the other hand, it seemed to confirm that some sort of offense had been committed by the victims.

Once deciphered, the meaning of the communiqué seemed to be that reprisals had been taken against people who had involved themselves with the underground press. This explanation was not far from the truth; the murder victims included the wealthy baker Blaiman, who had subsidized this effort. And E. Kagan was always pulling mimeographed bulletins out of his pockets—foreign radio news he would then recite. No doubt the Germans had informers in the ghetto. For those of us who interacted with large numbers of the population through our constant attendance at meetings, the situation had become dangerous.

Obviously, the *Judenrat* could have no influence over the course of events: it was unable either to hinder or change anything. The *Judenrat* certainly did not want to plunder the Jews by taking their warm clothing from them, and the assassinations of April 17 had moved the majority of its members as much as the other inhabitants of the ghetto. But the latter event was often used as a pretext by the *Judenrat* in its efforts to gain control over and stifle independent political activity in the ghetto. In any case, these randomly chosen facts confirm the notion that the *Judenräte* were instruments of German policy and directly carried out Germans' orders or served as their mouthpiece.

Nevertheless, the *Judenräte* cannot be considered organs of collaboration. The term "collaboration," in the meaning we came to give it during the Second World War, includes the granting by the Germans of a certain liberty, however minimal, to the individuals and circles sought out by them for voluntary collaboration. For the *Judenräte* this dimension never existed. In this sense, the German policy toward the Jews in no way differed from that applied to the country as a whole. The press often refers to Poland as a "country without Quislings," words which became a slogan and were spoken with pride.

It is difficult, in general, to imagine a country that does not contain a small group of traitors ready to take power from the hand of the cruelest occupying force: and this applies above all to Poland, which, in the prewar years, was systematically poisoned by anti-semitic and totalitarian venom and whose leaders received Goebbels, Goering, and Frank as distinguished guests.

If Poland was the "country without Quislings," it was because the Germans never looked for any. They did not want to create even the illusion of a Polish government, and were content to subjugate the Polish administration by using it to carry out their policies. The *Judenräte* played the same role, but in even more bald and blatant fashion.

Yet at the same time there is another very important aspect to the role and activity of the *Judenräte* in Poland, particularly in Warsaw. Having crammed the Jews into the enclosure of the ghetto, the Germans generally took little interest in them and interfered relatively little with the life and internal relations of the Jewish population. In effect, then, full powers were delegated to the *Judenrat*. To the extent it could in this city of death, the *Judenrat* was free to regulate and govern the life of the Jews.

This is why, before the judgment of posterity, the *Judenrat* must bear full responsibilities for its acts and its failings in this area. It was responsible for the activities of the Jewish police, which was subordinate to it and transformed itself into a mob of gangsters; for the corruption that penetrated all the organizations it directed, and for much else besides. But the main thing for which the Warsaw *Judenrat* is to be blamed is its abiding indifference to the atrocious sufferings of the masses and its refusal to take those measures that were within its power to alleviate even a bit of the misery of the most helpless inhabitants of the ghetto.

Few people are aware that, in the first years of the occupation, on the basis of demands that all Jews up to the age of sixty be subject to obligatory labor, the Germans organized, in various places across Poland, small, Jewish work or "education" camps. In springtime in every ghetto they would take a certain number of people, young for the most part, and keep them until the autumn, at which point they could go home. These camps were often organized separately for the Jews of each city, so that there existed a camp for the Jews of Warsaw, another for the Jews of Lublin, etc. They were run by the SS. These were not yet extermination camps, but it would be fair to call them torture camps. Words cannot describe the sufferings and humiliations the victims had to endure. Nutrition was such that every prisoner suffered from dysentery. Despite this, after a certain hour, it was forbidden to leave the camp barracks. The SS would shoot point-blank anyone who tried to leave. The filth and stench, hunger and terror that reigned in the camps were indescribable. Many victims lacked the strength to endure such a life and left it to their fellow prisoners to dig their graves. Yet I did see some who returned. A doctor from the OSE* showed me a young man whose whole body was covered with scabies. The doctor told me that he could never before have imagined a sick person left in so neglected a state. I had occasion to speak with a group of young people who had returned from a camp in the autumn of 1941. Some of them had volunteered for it, considering that, since it was inevitable, it was their duty not to create complications and, by their example, cooperate in forming a contingent. I had known two of these young people before—they had been quite lively and robust. Both boys, to say nothing of the traces of beatings they bore, now gave the impression of being people drained of their vital forces. After the ordeal they had been through, they had no strength left to go on living. Several of them died soon after.

In this period, all these horrors were not part of some well-ordered program arranged by the authorities, but rather they occurred on a local scale. The living conditions of the prisoners thus depended, to a great extent, on the goodwill of the supervising SS, whose rank in the administrative hierarchy was not very high and who could be made more conciliatory through gifts and money, all the more since the Germans saw no objection to having the communities the prisoners came from exercise protection over them. I knew of cases where the delegates of provincial *Judenräte* would visit the camps, bring medicines, and, having made deals with the SS administration, obtain improvements in living conditions, replacing the weak or elderly with those younger

---

* Oeuvre de Secourse aux Enfants, relocated from Berlin to Paris in 1933. [Translator's note]

or more robust, and even reducing in the number of prisoners. The Warsaw *Judenrat* used none of these means and, once its contingent had left for the labor camp, showed no concern for the prisoners' fate. The one time the delegates were to visit the camp, they backed off. Thus the inmates from Warsaw were much worse off than natives of other towns.

My readers must understand what a heavy task falls to the chronicler of the Vanished City: the just and the guilty, the victims and those whose hearts were closed to the sufferings of their brethren, all died as martyrs in the total extermination; almost no one remains to be blamed for the past. To conceive and tell such a story, one must leave aside all personal elements. But it seems to me that the unparalleled tragedy of the life and disappearance of this ephemeral city compels a narrator to tell the whole truth and avoid none of the darker aspects of ghetto life. There were many—and how could it have been otherwise? In a human society under such terrible conditions, flung into chaos, wickedness and total defenselessness, distress and misfortune, when a fierce struggle was required just to maintain one's very physical existence, the basest instincts at times necessarily gained the upper hand and allowed only those without scruples to stay on top. What is much more surprising (and is a happy exception to the normal course of things) is that in the Warsaw ghetto, alongside the dark forces and despite and against all that was taking place, broad and much more numerous sectors of the Jewish population kept their high human standards intact. Far from turning numb or bestial, they took care not only of themselves but also of their neighbors, were ready to sacrifice themselves for them, and had created large-scale philanthropic institutions in forms unparalleled elsewhere. It is my fundamental task to give at least a sense of those institutions that confronted the ghetto's central problem, which was social as well as moral.

If, therefore, I have been further obliged to make mention of the *Judenrat,* it is only insofar as its response to such problems influenced the life of the ghetto. In particular, it is not my intention to go into the whole matter of the Warsaw *Judenrat*'s taxation policy, but only to illustrate by various examples to what extent the ghetto's life was made even more painful by the council's indifference to the sufferings of the hapless residents of the Refugee Centers, or of those who died of inanition, or a slow, painful death in the ghetto streets, or in their dirty, narrow dwellings.

In this fundamental problem of ghetto life, the population was left to its own devices and met with neither help nor understanding on the part of the administration.

IV. THE SOCIAL STRUCTURE OF THE GHETTO

Much has been made of the social contrasts found in the ghetto, although they exist in various forms all over the world, and the Warsaw ghetto was surely not the place to achieve perfect social justice. But in this hermetically-sealed universe, which constituted, so to speak, a testing ground, all vital functions were performed on a higher, starker, more brutal plane: the social contrast did not reside in the imbalance between a laborer's wages and the fantastic income of an industrial magnate, nor in the opposition between hut and palace. It appeared in a more elementary way: in the difference between those who ate their fill and those who starved—as was glaringly evident to the crowds of beggars dying of hunger, who wandered streets that had their share of restaurants and cafés serving the choicest fare.

The main boulevard of the ghetto, Leszno Street, could boast at least twenty restaurants; there were as many, however, on Zelazna Street, Siena Street, and elsewhere. Given the general poverty, young girls and women from all sorts of backgrounds offered their services as waitresses. Managers had quite a choice, then, and no city in the world had as many beautiful and elegant women serving in cafés as did the short-lived ghetto, with its Café des Arts, Splendid, Negresco, etc.

The premises of some of these establishments were tastefully decorated, the food was good and plentiful, and the window displays with their wine bottles and various hors d'oeuvres were highly enticing. But right in front of these display windows, hordes of wretched beggars would pass, often collapsing from inanition. Seeing them, I would wonder why these wretched souls, who after all had nothing to lose, didn't smash those windows, grab something from them, and at last appease their hunger! As far as I know, though, nothing of the sort happened. People resigned to hunger died slow deaths in front of restaurants and grocery stores. Why? Neither fear nor thrashings from the Jewish police stopped them, but rather the hopelessness of their situation. The ghetto was supplied clandestinely and, despite the semblance of abundance, food was in fact so scarce that, if one had evenly distributed the restaurants' supplies, they would not have sufficed to offer a single meal to all the starving. Life in this sealed coffin had its own laws and inflicted on its victims continual sufferings that often enough ended in death.

Our circle of community workers was painfully affected by this aspect of ghetto life, and the cry sometimes went up to have all restaurants and cafés closed. It was a solution our feelings naturally inclined us toward, but hardly addressed the real issue. The closing of restaurants would not have improved the situation of the hungry, it would merely have swelled their numbers, since a great many workers were employed by these establishments and their suppliers.

Given the more than cramped conditions of the ghetto's apartments, for many the hours spent talking with friends in a café or restaurant were the only moments of relaxation. I am not speaking of dives like the Hotel Britannia, at 20 Nowolipie Street, or meeting places for the more dubious elements, but of ordinary establishments. These were just like those of any other city in the world. They gave the illusion of the normal life from which the Jews had been severed. And their continued existence in a city which the Germans regarded as a cemetery—was it not, in a certain sense, the ghetto's protest, its affirmation of the right to life?

When, through a combination of hard work and taste, some dusty ghetto courtyard was transformed into a café in a garden with grass, flowers, and even a small fountain; when some of these establishments offered a musical program of high artistic merit; when orchestras played English songs (which was inconceivable in any other area under German occupation), was this not proof of the ghetto's vitality?

One day the German chief of police for the ghetto, [Heinz] Auerswald, entered unnoticed into one of the cafés on Leszno Street and heard English being sung. He was seized with such rage that he threatened to have the whole place destroyed. But in fact the incident passed without consequences—the owners no doubt having managed to "appease" the police chief.

The only solution to the problem of the striking contrast between affluence and hunger, so rankling to our consciences, would have been to force the rich to share with the hungry. But one couldn't expect a gesture of compassion on the part of the nouveaux riches racking up their astronomical bills in the restaurants; these were people without scruple, who had often acquired their fortunes by dubious means. Never before in any society has their breed of men taken pity on the misery of others. Here is one cruel story that will give an idea of their heartlessness:

A bigshot, self-satisfied, is seated before a copious spread of food. A weary beggar, covered in rags, manages to approach his table and asks for alms; he is refused. The beggar persists, pleading that he has had nothing to eat in two days. To which the rich man replies: "That's the limit! It's not enough that he doesn't eat himself, but he won't let anyone else eat in peace either!"

The only authority able to subdue people of this sort and force them to do their duty was the *Judenrat*, or more precisely, its food-supply department. This institution was led by former members of the Jewish Shopkeepers' Union, who, in exercising their functions, could not quite get beyond the mentality of their milieu. The people who approached them told me that they considered it their most important task to promote the development of commerce and the profitability of the ghetto's commercial enterprises.

At the head of this group was Abram Hepner, seventy years old, formerly president of the Shopkeepers' Union and, in the ghetto, a member of the *Judenrat* and its minister of supplies. Hepner was quite a remarkable figure. He was a self-made man who had built up an important metal-selling business, organized largely around the needs of its employees. He was a scrupulously honest man, ready to sacrifice himself to do his duty as he understood it. At the time of mass deportations, when roundups and selections extended to the officials too, he automatically placed himself first among his colleagues in the ranks out of which they had begun choosing victims.

Unfortunately, this man lacked modesty, in Camus's sense of the term, which implies taking the views of others into account. He would settle all questions on his own and brooked no objections or criticism. The very idea of public supervision struck him as a personal offense. Under these conditions, the predictable thing happened: power was given to the flunkies who knew best how to play up to their master. Hepner's main collaborator in the area of general supplies was a corrupt man, and in the area of mutual aid it was Henry Rottenberg, an honest and upright, but ambitious and authoritarian young man.

I think it is an invariable principle that any unchecked authority, once it commits an error, never retreats, and one error is enough to set it on a relentlessly downward path.

This is what happened in the ghetto's supplies department: its disorder and corruption rose exponentially, and although Hepner continued to command general respect, his activities aroused mounting discontent among the socially aware. I recall that at one meeting of the Main Commission (the higher branch of social services, founded shortly before July 1942 and made up of the representatives of political parties, several different institutions, and the Central Commission of Tenement Committees), someone named Neustadt voiced vehement protests against a series of measures taken by Hepner. In the commission, however, this Neustadt, one of the directors of the AJDC, [American Joint Distribution Committee], represented the *Centos* (Central Society for the Protection of Orphans), an institution sponsored and supported by none other than Hepner.

Hepner viewed himself as the protector of Jewish children. His motto was generous and heroic: "Our children must live." Fulfilling this slogan, however, depended on the *Centos*. Before the war this had been an important social institution, financed primarily by the AJDC, which made a large-scale commitment to the care of orphans. At the time of the occupation, it was administered by two directors, who transformed it into an organization protecting children in general, a field in which it now claimed a monopoly.

The protection of children represents another sad aspect of ghetto life. As it is a topic that warrants fuller discussion than I can give it, let me just cite one illustration, a strange measure that was adopted. For a plate of soup in the people's kitchen, an adult without means would have to pay, in addition to the price, which would be about fifty groschen, a supplement of twenty to twenty-five groschen, to reduce the price paid by children. In this way, the feeding of children was funded not by the rich but by the poor! The essential error here came, however, from the fact that, in practice, only a small privileged group had the right to be identified as "our children": those who had been lucky enough to be admitted into children's centers! The great majority of the others went without any protection whatsoever, whereas the "boarders" were often set up rather comfortably and lived in comparative luxury. When community welfare groups (the women's circles of the Mutual Aid Sector) tried to conduct relief work on behalf of the most abject of the unsheltered children, whom no one took care of, they met with various obstacles, because their efforts infringed upon the authority of the *Centos*. But the efforts of social organizations to change this policy were doomed because of the support lent to the *Centos* by Hepner and other influential members of the *Judenrat*.

The directors of the *Centos*—Adolf Berman and Jozef Gitler—both of whom, I'm happy to say, survived, have surely not forgotten the objections and criticisms formulated by the office of the Central Commission of Tenement Committees on many occasions, but particularly at the time of our meetings organized in the apartment of the engineer Zabludowski.

For the entire lifespan of the ghetto, groups dedicated to social relief, or really social rescue, disagreed with the representatives of the authorities. After lengthy appeals, the *Judenrat* had finally published an ordinance placing a 10 percent tax on all restaurant checks, to go to mutual aid; but this collection had to be carried out under the supervision of *Judenrat* agents who were not always impervious to the tangible arguments the restaurateurs could offer. All the measures carried out so that the collection and supervision of the tax could be done by Mutual Aid (*ZTOS.*),* which had honest, dedicated staffs in the Public Sector, were unsuccessful. In the end this more than modest tax was never lawfully collected.

It is clear that the tax represented only a partial measure; only in a limited way did it resolve a problem that needed to be viewed in far broader terms. All those with adequate means should have contributed to compensate for the most flagrant injustices, and to ease, even temporarily and partially, the fate of the most abject of the population.

It must be borne in mind, however, that implementing our suggestions for a general tax on all capital and income along the principles of any other civil society met with great difficulties here by virtue of the ghetto's specific social structure.

Among the inhabitants of the Warsaw ghetto, two basic groups must first be distinguished:

1) those who had lived there previously and who owned businesses in the territory later assigned to the ghetto; and

---

* *Zydowskie Towarystwo Opieki Spoleczacj,* or Jewish Mutual Aid Society. [Translator's note.]

2) the inhabitants of other parts of the city, who were compelled to settle there. (I do not count the third category here—the inhabitants of the nearby areas later integrated into the ghetto, the poor who were registered with social relief.)

The situation of people in the first group was generally more favorable, for they got to live in their own former apartments and essentially to go about their usual lives; the new arrivals were deprived of all that. Officially, they were allowed to bring only personal effects into the ghetto, since all their furnishings were to be given to Aryans. In actual fact, it was possible in most cases to bring furniture too, though there was no place to put it. For example, when my wife and I moved into the ghetto, there was room in our one-room dwelling for only a couch, two armchairs, and a part of my library.

The shopkeepers who had businesses at the street level had preserved, despite the looting that immediately followed the occupation, a large part of their merchandise and could therefore use it one way or another. The owners of businesses outside the ghetto, on the other hand, had in most cases lost all their goods, having been quite simply driven out of their premises and forced to give up their keys; or else they had all merchandise confiscated. Sometimes, to keep this from occurring, they transferred their stocks to Poles, but never managed to recover them.

The Jews were divested of owning and managing their industries and businesses, as well as of their real estate, which was turned over to special German institutions or to administrators appointed by those institutions. Jews' bank accounts and stocks were frozen. Thus, the Jews were stripped of all the normal elements of private means that serve as a basis for taxation.

Jews' private means thus consisted of those liquid assets, foreign stocks, and precious gems the Germans had not discovered and confiscated. In this way certain families retained large fortunes that were hard to assess for tax purposes.

Generally the well-to-do simply spent their savings. The percentage of those who earned their living in the ghetto was far lower than in any other human society. Nonetheless, there existed and arose groups who continued to earn large sums of money and even to become rich. Among them were those merchants who made use of their existing businesses or created new ones, especially the sort that served the most basic needs of the population: grocery stores, restaurants, bakeries. There were, for example, many very wealthy bakers and confectioners as well as brush manufacturers for the Germans, who never ceased increasing their fortunes.

Consequently a new sort of profiteer emerged, who made huge profits by exploiting specific conditions in ghetto life. These included big-time smugglers, those who had obtained German concessions to sell certain merchandise or to use certain means of communication (Kohn & Heller), Jewish subcontractors who filled the orders of German firms, members of the department of supplies who held franchises on production of the most essential commodities, such as jam or artificial honey, and who could procure sugar at fixed prices, etc . . . .

This at-best-cursory analysis of the ghetto's social structure reveals that the ghetto contained elements who might easily have made sacrifices on behalf of the needy, but could not easily be made to do so. The difficulties were not insurmountable, however; information provided by experts in every branch and by the Tenement Committees could have served as the basis for applying severe but fair measures that fulfilled a basic moral duty. Yet the *Judenrat* refused to pursue this path: it allowed either indirect taxes on staples, or direct taxes, equal for everyone, which crushed poor people while barely inconveniencing the rich.

Under ghetto conditions, moreover, these taxes were thoroughly inadequate to amass the necessary funds. Some examples of this social policy included: 10 percent of commodities distributed to holders of food cards was taken out for social assistance, meaning that the poor were deprived of their last piece of bread; a general tax, the same for everyone, was established for combatting epidemics; the "Month of the Child" was marked by a series of mandatory collections, again at one fixed amount for everyone; medicines were assigned a tax representing 40 percent of their value, and so on. In addition, the *Judenrat* had instituted a tax of one zloty for the monthly renewal of every food card. Despite violent protests, the *Judenrat* never saw fit to repeal this measure; much later, it agreed to increase the amount, in individual cases, to between two and five zlotys, but it never actually carried out this modification. Since a great many ghetto residents were without any means whatsoever, and, on the other hand, the *Judenrat* could not deprive them of food cards, these people were exempted from the tax and received special stubs which gave them the right to obtain food cards for free.

No one who did not himself live in the Warsaw ghetto can imagine what a sinister shadow these stubs cast over the life of the ghetto, and what hellish struggles broke out when they were distributed. At first, they were given out directly by the *Judenrat,* but the abuses were such that the Council preferred to turn this function over to Mutual Aid. Not that the clamor ended there, at its Central Office. Only much later was a new system devised: the Central Office gave out the available quantity of stubs, based on a set coefficient, over six districts, which distributed them through the Tenement Committees. But the number of stubs was always insufficient, since the number the *Judenrat* issued was always smaller than that of the needy. Every month the districts were literally besieged by frantic crowds of indigents who had not received stubs. Thus, until July 1942, "Rozensztat's famine tax" (the name was inspired by the tax's creator, an influential member of the *Judenrat*) weighed heavily on the ghetto and was the source of much alarm and unrest. When the *Große Aktion* started up, these same stubs turned into death warrants, certificates guaranteeing you a speedy death. The mass deportations began with the residents of Refugee Centers; next came the poorest housing blocks, the occupants' state of indigence being established by the number of stubs they had been granted. I do not know if this plan was devised by the Jewish police or if they were merely following German orders, but in any case the psychological wager behind it was right: the holders of stubs, driven to despair, offered no resistance to deportation.

It is interesting to note that even when the Official Aid Committee (*KOM*) took the trouble to reflect more deeply on how to solve this social problem, without drawing on the private means or incomes of citizens, it never managed to break out of the vicious circle of food cards.

So it happened that in the spring of 1941 the demagogic plan was launched to confiscate the food cards of well-to-do Jews; in other words, to transfer their share of card-rationed goods to mutual aid institutions. Since enforcing this measure required the participation of the Tenement Committees, no one dared to apply it without the consent of the

Public Sector. In April 1941, the Official Aid Committee submitted for approval by the Central Commission of Tenement Committees a plan to confiscate 30,000 food cards. After a thorough study of the project at a general meeting, the commission rejected it. Among other reasons was the risk of alerting the Germans that some Jews could do without food cards, though anywhere else in the world the adoption of such a card system was meant for universal use, with no exceptions. If I am not mistaken, this same resolution contained our suggestions concerning measures that could be adopted in place of such cheap demagoguery. Though the plan to confiscate food cards was subsequently shelved, our positive suggestions were never considered.

One single important measure had been put into effect, and that was the creation of a special commission (*Momisja Przesidelencza*), which acted nominally on behalf of the *Judenrat*, but actually conducted its activity in the offices of the Official Aid Committee and of Mutual Aid with the help of workers from both institutions.

The task of the commission was to implement an extraordinary tax on the wealthy. The amount of taxation per person was established on the basis of confidential data, decisions being made at closed meetings; no taxpayer would be allowed to lodge a complaint. The decisions were to be final and to be implemented without delay. The sanction for nonpayment was the transfer of the taxpayer to a Refugee Center. The meaning of this measure was clear: anyone unwilling to help his less fortunate brothers would have to share in their existence and be made to appreciate their sufferings.

The measures adopted by this commission obviously had a certain effectiveness, yet opinion about them in the Public Sector was divided. I refused to participate in them, and would be rebuked for this even by my closest colleagues. In my opinion, working along such principles could not guarantee fair and equable taxation; I thought it necessary to set up a more general tax guided by more standard principles, and I felt that the taxpayers did have a right to make appeals, etc. People's rebuttal to this argument was that desperate times demanded desperate remedies.

Today, the question is not whether one side was right or wrong; the controversy sheds light, rather, on the ideological processes of that vanished world. I must admit that, on this issue, I was in a minority, and several remarkable figures in the Public Sector played an active part in the commission. Among them was Alexander Landau, a man of unforgettable merit. Bighearted, radiant in mind and spirit, he was a superb organizer, epitomizing the sort of practical idealism that conceives every idea in terms of actual goals, and thus always attains maximum efficacy. Alexander Landau was, so to speak, always in the front lines of community work. One day, when the ghetto's borders were changed, it happened that an entire apartment block was cut off from the outer world; its residents faced starvation. It was Landau who, despite all obstacles, found the means to get into these apartments and supply them with food. He was one of the organizers and directors of the Toporol Society (Society for Agricultural Development), whose goal was to make use of every inch of free land, every courtyard and every balcony, to grow grass, plants, and vegetables. These efforts served at the same time as gardening courses for young people. Landau was one of the leaders of the left-wing Zionist youth and even in the ghetto continued training cadres for Israel.

From the outset he helped to organize people's kitchens and Tenement Committees and was a permanent board member of the Central Commission of Tenement Committees.

He and his brother owned a small carpentry shop on Gesia Street, which, once the mass deportations began, served as a refuge for community workers.

It is here in Paris that I received posthumous news of Alexander Landau. In 1943 he had been transferred to Vittel*. I had occasion to see the notes he had dictated there, in a tense, fitful style, about life and social work in Warsaw.

He had lost his only daughter, who had met with a heroic death in Warsaw, and he himself died a martyr, after making his last journey from Vittel to an extermination camp in Poland.

In the area of public instruction, the *Judenrat* had demonstrated a greater understanding of the needs of the ghetto population. This task may well have been facilitated for the Council by the activity of J. Jaszunski, a very energetic man and the former director of the Polish ORT [Organization for Rehabilitation Training], and who, if I'm not mistaken, became a member and vice-president of the *Judenrat*. Though I was quite far removed from this domain, I know that a series of courses of general instruction and professional training had been organized. Courses in medicine were also set up and, shortly before the month of July 1942, a whole clandestine polytechnic school was being planned. The implementation of this last project had been entrusted

---

* Vittel, a former spa in the Vosges, near Nancy, was used to detain relatively protected persons, either those thought suitable for exchange, or holders of Latin American documents. Nevertheless, in 1944, hundreds of Jews were sent from there to the transit camp at Drancy, and onward to extermination at Auschwitz. [Translator's note.]

to my friend, the engineer Raphael Buchweitz, who kept me abreast of its progress. Since, as far as I know, the name of this remarkable man has not entered into any publication about the ghetto, I would like these few lines in his memory to serve as a modest monument for his unmarked grave.

Buchweitz was a cultured man and, as rarely happens, his competence extended both to the exact sciences and the humanities: a mathematician and metallurgist, he was also a philosopher and historian. In his practical life he had devoted himself to professional training; in any other country his activity would have taken place on a grand scale, but in Poland, he had to be content with directing a private Jewish professional school, whose very high level was of his creation. On a modest salary, paid sporadically, he had managed to build up a very fine library for himself. It was his sole wealth, and he was deeply attached to it. With the creation of the ghetto, he eked out a difficult existence, and sometimes he and his wife had nothing more to eat than soup once a day. I recall that one day when I ran into him, he showed me, with a sad smile, two volumes of Laplace's works, bound in red leather, which he was selling to the book dealer for a mere pittance.

This man possessed such spontaneous optimism, such reserves of inner strength, that his courage never abandoned him. His creative energy prevented him from ever imagining destructive processes. I was in his office on Leszno Street when the *Große Aktion* began, and even at that moment he was busy with his work, preparing his curriculum for the polytechnic school.

He and his wife survived the first wave of mass deportations. Later, his wife, a small, delicate creature, committed suicide by taking poison, whereas he, my sources told me, survived a while longer after being conscripted into a German unit. He was killed by the Germans a few weeks after their retreat from Poland.

Still, despite the importance of public instruction, neither it nor any other forward-looking cultural project could offset the ghetto's basic social problem. In a milieu in which death by starvation was a daily phenomenon for entire families and Refugee Centers, all social energy had to be channeled into the struggle against this horrific reality. Such a struggle had to encompass the broadest strata of the population: no one could remain indifferent. The Public Sector of Mutual Aid had taken up the task of mobilizing the whole society to participate in this struggle. The dynamism of the masses it managed to create stands as moral justification for the ghetto of 1940–42, both for itself and for future generations.

V. THE GHETTO'S SOCIAL INSTITUTIONS

The committees elected in all residential buildings can be considered the basic cells of the Public Sector. From these committees, whether by vote or natural selection, there arose different commissions in every district (some were set up to oversee the Tenement Committees, others to collect funds, etc.). At the head of this organization was the Central Commission—the parliament of the Public Sector. At the time this commission bore a rather untranslateable name, the *Komisja Miedzydzielnicowa,* which is why it appears in the present narrative as the "Central Commission of Tenement Committees," corresponding to the functions and role it was called upon to play.

To give a clearer sense of the Public Sector's activity, let me first give a brief sketch of the general organization of social welfare in occupied Poland, which will help to explain the Sector's work.

From the start of the occupation, the Germans created one organ for social welfare for the entire population (including the Jews) that went by the name of the Central Assistance Council (*Rada Glowna Opiekuncza*), based in Cracow. Funds were allocated to the various nationalities according to a certain preestablished scheme, with approximately 80 percent allotted to the Poles, 15 percent to the Ukrainians, and 5 percent to the Jews. This disproportionate distribution obviously represented a prejudice against the Jews, and I am not sure, for that matter, that this tiny portion was ever in fact distributed. At the start of the occupation and even during the early period after the consolidation into the ghetto, the representatives of official Jewish welfare attended the meetings, in Cracow, which were led by Governor General Frank's secretary of state for welfare. I was told that at the outset, faced with the sheer impossibility of opposing anti-Jewish measures, the Jewish representatives nevertheless dared to protest in the course of these meetings against the abuses committed in excess of these measures.

Such protests would have been absolutely unthinkable even shortly after. The dizzying escalation of Hitler's atrocities was only in part the inevitable result of their bestiality once unleashed; through their premeditated policy the Nazis also tried to persuade the German people that they had no choice but to fight to the death, since, in the event of defeat, all Germans without exception would bear responsibility for crimes perpetrated in their name. I remember quite clearly a series of articles by Goebbels in the magazine *Das Reich,* which aimed to inculcate this idea in the Germans.

On the local level, each nationality's social welfare system functioned separately. The Jews had the Official Aid Committee (*KOM*), which in Warsaw was directed by the engineer Stanislaw Szereszewski, an affluent industrialist who before the war had kept his distance from the social activities of the Jewish community. He was an intelligent, hardworking, and loyal man. I often had occasion to discuss various issues with him, and in every instance we were able to find a mutually acceptable solution.

Another member of the *KOM* was the director of the AJDJ, Isaac Giterman, whose activities I was familiar with as far back as the First World War, when he was in Kiev, with the Relief Committee for Austrian Jewish Refugees and Hostages. His activities between the wars and during the occupation were a credit to the Jews of Poland. We were often brought together through our work in the ghetto, and Giterman gave several reports to the Central Commission of Tenement Committees. He perished in 1943, still full of strength and energy, when he could have continued and expanded his activity in postwar conditions.

In keeping with German plans, the *KOM* was chosen to become the sole organization for Jewish welfare work, absorbing and supplanting all others. In this way the latter were expected to lose their particular character and autonomy, and thus doomed to vanish into the single, homogeneous *KOM* organism.

I do not have sufficient documentation to trace the activity of the *KOM* in all its aspects, but I must point out one of its great merits: instead of exploiting the official monopoly conferred upon it, it limited its role to the allocating of funds among the other institutions and to dealing with the Germans in matters of relief work; thus, all the other institutions were able, in fact, to preserve their autonomy and perform their work effectively.

This situation changed, however, after the dismissal of the engineer Szereszewski in the spring of 1942 and the appointment to the *KOM* presidency of the lawyer Gustaw Wielikowski. He was a member of the *Judenrat*, the head of its social services, and at the same time a counselor (*Berater*) to the German governor of Warsaw in welfare questions or Jewish affairs in general—I can't recall his exact title. A talented lawyer and orator, Wielikowski was unfortunately not a man to follow the straight and narrow path in his work.

The need to merge institutions into the *KOM* was presented to us as a categorical demand by the Germans. We had no possibility of checking if this was true. At this time a series of meetings took place in which I happened to participate; they were devoted to discussions of the new methods for our activity, for even Wielikowski didn't dare to just start tampering with highly competent social institutions. We were forced to accept the merger of institutions as a basis for negotiations, but it was stipulated that a higher organ of social assistance, to whose directives the *KOM* would be subservient, would be set up under the name of "Main Commission" (I have already described its makeup in the previous chapter). The planning of statutes for the Main Commission and its relations with the *K.O.M.* was entrusted to Zisze Frydman, leader of the *Agudah*.* Fridman was a man with a luminous mind and spirit, and the loyalty and probity of his character were exceptional.

On reading through Frydman's plan, I was literally dazzled by its exactness, its logic, and at the same time its conciseness. I remember instantly feeling happy about it, and saying that if ever, in my career as a lawyer, I were having trouble formulating a complicated legal document, I would turn to him for advice. Alas! in the light of subsequent events every word uttered in the ghetto, even in jest, takes on a tragic character. Zisze Frydman disappeared amid great upheaval and was never to have the chance to serve his people, either by good deeds or by his valuable counsel. In the Pantheon of the Warsaw Ghetto, his name deserves a place of honor.

Wielikowski's attitude toward Frydman's plan was, as ever, ambiguous: on the one hand, he accepted the principle that

* *Agudah*, or *Agudat Israel*, was a political party of the Orthodox, founded in 1912. [Translator's note.]

the social element, as personified by the Main Commission, should be paramount; but, on the other hand, he tried, by incredible subterfuges, to stall on implementing the plan and to cripple its importance by proposing various modifications.

All his procrastination continued into July 1942; and thus, by force of circumstance, for the whole first phase of the ghetto's existence, right up until the start of mass exterminations that fateful month (i.e., when the community had risen to some 400,000 inhabitants), its social institutions functioned independently—both those that had existed before (*OSE, Centos*) as well as the main organ of social welfare created at the start of the occupation and named *ZTOS*. (Jewish Mutual Aid Society), later shortened to *ZOS* (Jewish Mutual Aid). We shall refer to it simply as Mutual Aid.

The administrative apparatus of Mutual Aid had several different elements, but among them were a large number of people who demonstrated an intense dedication to community work. The names of most of them have slipped my mind, but I would like to mention here one of the most praiseworthy—the lawyer Moishe Kaganowicz. After the First World War he collaborated closely with Isaac Grinbaum on the National Jewish Council (which was created at that time in Poland). He remained a staunch supporter and member of the Zionist movement. In all his work, both before the war and during the occupation, he radiated nobility of character, modesty, and dedication to social causes. He was deliberately self-effacing and devoted himself selflessly to the work of Mutual Aid. Incidentally, this did not always save him from clashes with the bureaucratic elements of this institution. Indeed, one fairly typical instance of this springs to mind:

With a colleague by the name of Lebenhaft, Kaganowicz was directing the service that gave the needy coupons good for meals at the people's kitchens. The kitchens, however, were run by a special service.

This division of functions had been made on the principle that running kitchens fell within the sphere of economic organization, whereas distributing coupons to different groups or individuals was a social operation and thus a matter for the Public Sector.

One day, the head of kitchen services, Szpindler, who incidentally was a loyal and conscientious man, staged a coup d'état: without warning, he decreed an audit on all distributed coupons, and validated only those that he himself deemed necessary. Kaganowicz called on my help, and I submitted the matter to the Central Commission of Tenement Committees for deliberation. Although his functions placed Szpindler out of our realm, he came to the meeting. This fact was symptomatic of the authority the Central Commission enjoyed as the only organization in the ghetto acting on the principles of free representative institutions.

After a prolonged and tumultuous debate, the commission adopted a resolution fully upholding Kaganowicz's position and, as far as I can remember, laid out a course of action that both services could accept.

Mutual Aid provided relief services for refugees. It ran the Centers and took care of collection and distribution of clothing. The first clothing drives had been quite successful, but subsequently this service lost some of its importance.

The most important service was obviously that of the people's kitchens. About these kitchens one can make the following observations:

1) The quantity of meals distributed varied over different periods but was always insufficient;

2) The kitchens functioned irregularly and intermittently; food shortages sometimes forced them to close their doors. I remember our joy when, after a long closing, we would receive a large shipment of oats, meant specifically for them. The kitchens then resumed giving out soup;

3) It was hard to combat misappropriations. Abuse was not widespread, but despite the inadequacy of the diet—theoretically two grams of fat per person—a part was diverted by the personnel to feed their own hungry families. All these facts and the measures adopted to combat them were reported by Szpindler at one of the last meetings of the Central Commission of Tenement Committees, which took up the question at his initiative. Certain kitchens, organized and supervised by community workers in the Public Sector, functioned more satisfactorily. Among these I can cite by memory: 23 Nalewski Street (founded by E. Kagan), 15 Twarda Street (founded by Alexander Landau), and 22 Leszno Street (founded by Sukiennik, Braun, and Cholewa);

4) What was most tragic, however, was the fact that the food distributed by the kitchens was thoroughly insufficient to keep a human being alive. Those who had to settle for this amount could not survive for long. Once a day the kitchens dished out a soup that was often quite thin. After having absorbed this low-calorie nourishment for a long time, the digestive organs ceased to function normally. Dysentery was rampant and quickly led already debilitated people to the grave.

Generally, though, I should say that if Mutual Aid's activities were not without flaws, and if Mutual Aid has occasionally been criticized for a certain bureaucratic excess, it nonetheless performed a genuine service for the most deprived.

In addition to its official activity, Mutual Aid became the rallying center for all those vital forces in the Public Sector that had been stirred to take social action and formed cadres of volunteer social workers numbering in the thousands.

The Public Sector itself consisted of two branches: on the one hand, it had an official administrative apparatus, which, from an organizational standpoint, formed a Mutual Aid service subordinate to it. At its head was Doctor Ringelblum, the force behind our whole movement, and its most creative mind.

On the other hand, the Public Sector was made up of thousands of volunteer community workers, who formed, as I have mentioned: 1) committees in all tenement buildings; 2) various commissions in all districts, with affiliated groups of relief workers, women's circles, etc.; and, finally, 3) the Central Commission of Tenement Committees, created at the end of 1940, and serving as a sort of parliament for the Public Sector.

Initially Dr. Ringelblum intended to limit voluntary social work to the district level and to direct such work through his central apparatus. This attitude had somewhat delayed the formation of the Central Commission, but once it was organized, Ringelblum was the first to appreciate its importance. He did not miss a single session, and the collaboration of the commission with the administrative apparatus of the Sector ran perfectly smoothly, from a shared effort to mobilize as much goodwill as was available. In its gradual evolution, this official administrative machine eventually became the executive organ of the Public Sector. Doctor Ringelblum would often say that he viewed himself as a prime minister of the Public Sector, responsible to his parliament. His closest colleagues were Eleazar Bloch, Meir Przedecz, Doctor Eck, and Starobinski.

All died martyrs' deaths,* and their names, except for that of Ringelblum, who enjoyed great posthumous popularity, will mean nothing to my readers. All are as much consigned to oblivion as the other victims of the Vanished City, but each of them had dedicated himself wholeheartedly to thankless rescue work and exerted so much effort under incredibly difficult circumstances that the fact of mentioning them here is but a faint echo of the memory they must have left in the hearts of our brethren who survived the catastrophe.

---

* With the happy exception of Dr. Eck, who, having been sent to Vittel, managed miraculously to save himself by jumping off the train during its stop at the Gare de l'Est in Paris.

VI. THE BIRTH AND EVOLUTION
OF TENEMENT COMMITTEES

In rudimentary form, tenement committees started up the moment the occupation began. The new living conditions, transforming the Jews into pariahs, created a psychological climate that could only favor their mutual reconciliation. Through the long winter evenings, the Jews could communicate only with residents of their own buildings, for the curfew started earlier for them than for the rest of the population: generally at 9:00 P.M., but in certain periods even at 7:00 P.M. In addition, the impending danger facing all Jews, the violence and lootings to which they were subjected, the sinister rumors of the fate that awaited them—all this bred the need to exchange ideas and to establish closer ties. In my own case, for example, I knew almost none of the neighbors in our building before the war; but with the onset of the hostilities, all the Jews left in our apartment building struck up acquaintances and were in constant contact with one another. Through this entirely natural need to unite and the necessity to remedy the plight of those Jews who had lost their incomes and means or had been ruined by lootings—and their numbers were always increasing—the general outlines of what would become the ghetto's Tenement Committees began to take shape.

The Tenement Committees established themselves as the ghetto's national institution. It would be a false interpretation of historical reality to credit their conception to any political party or individual.

Since I would like in these memoirs to avoid all polemics, I shall let that statement stand without elaborating on the efforts certain studies on the Warsaw ghetto have made to distort reality.

However, if one had to name one person who played a predominant role in this domain, it would surely be Doctor Ringelblum. Because he was the first to understand the importance of the Tenement Committees, he became their prime mover and architect, giving precise form to their organization and attracting to this endeavor groups of community workers—very few at first—those pioneers of the Public Sector whose work evolved, in the era of the ghetto, into a great popular movement.

Up until October 1940, Jews lived in every part of the city. At the time, Mutual Aid comprised eight sections (districts)—five of them were located in the quarters that had particularly dense Jewish populations and later formed part of the ghetto site; the Sixth comprised the right bank of the Vistula (the suburb of Praga); and the Seventh and Eighth, the south-west section, the wealthiest in Warsaw. As president of the Commission of Instruction and Inspection of the Tenement Committees, it was in this last district that I led efforts related to our organization. The Jewish population was less dense in this part of the city, and there weren't enough Jewish tenants in the houses for a committee to be formed in each building; thus, to reflect local conditions, we decided to organize the committees into blocs of three to ten houses each.

This was our working method: the streets of the district were divided among the members of the Commission; they would visit the houses assigned to them, get to know the residents, and take note of the active, capable people there who could be used for social work. Later, with the help of these data, we would map out the blocs; the representatives from each were then invited to a meeting in the district to form the bloc's committee; sometimes, propaganda meetings were organized in the apartment buildings, with all tenants invited. But committees would be formed only at the district meetings I would call together every day in the spring and summer of 1940, up until the month of September.

In this period, when the notion of Tenement Committees was still vague for most Jews, it was impossible to proceed by elections, and the ranks of committees were formed by selecting from the most active elements. All the daily meetings ended with forming of committees. I never encountered a single case of refusal, but that did not imply that the committee was ready to perform effective work. Once formed, the committees remained within our control. Some of them became vigorously active, but many of them showed inertia, providing therefore inadequate connections between the bloc's tenements. We made efforts to reinvigorate these committees with new members.

I can still remember one tumultuous meeting in the course of which the committee of a tenement bloc on Hoza Street was formed. At this time, Mutual Aid was taking up a clothing drive, and rumors had spread accusing certain contribution collectors of abuses (people were convinced they were replacing good-quality clothes with more worn-out ones). One of the people present at this meeting gave a violent speech confirming these accusations. As the Jews tend to be very sensitive to the flaws in their social institutions, this first speech set off a string of other speeches, even more vehement. The atmosphere heated up, and finally the assembly refused to collaborate with any institution as ineffectual as Mutual Aid.

At this moment I understood fully the justness of our system, whereby the volunteer community workers, and not the employees of Mutual Aid, took care of forming the committees. The latter would have been obliged to defend their institution, which would only have aggravated the situation. As for me, I could support an entirely different point of view, and I told these riled participants that, although I had no exact information, I did not deny the possibility of abuses (this was, moreover, my honest position). But if, for that reason, we decided to go home without undertaking any action, the only result would be an increase in abuses, for the sole means of combatting them was public supervision, a control we could only gain by influencing Mutual Aid with our own energetic social relief–work. At the end of my speech, a committee was formed without a single voice of dissent, and, as we would later observe, this committee was quite active.

Yet at this stage, the movement was still embryonic. It only took on its definite form and historic significance within the ghetto walls, where, due to the density and cohesion of the population, and unlike in the first period, committees were formed in every tenement building by electoral means.

The work of the Tenement Committees and the other institutions of the Public Sector that evolved out of them attracted the participation of all those forces that brought the greatest enthusiasm to the struggle against the horrible reality around us, and that kept up their activity even when they sometimes sensed the futility of their efforts and the hopelessness of resolving the social problem of the closed universe that was the Warsaw ghetto.

The Public Sector of Mutual Aid can be said unequivocally to have represented the will and conscience of the ghetto. People from every walk of life and every profession, as well as members of every political party, joined in its activities—people who had, at times, been quite active before the war but who, in the ghetto, had lost contact with their organizations. They came to work in our institutions not as representatives of their respective parties, but out of a spontaneous urge to help the destitute masses. The activity of these people of different persuasions, from the revisionists to the members of the *Bund,* took place in an atmosphere of brotherly solidarity, without a single misunderstanding created by opposing political opinions. The community workers of the Public Sector had obviously at times had different ideas about one issue or another, and often the discussions at meetings were violent, and yet those differences never reflected party loyalties.

The popular movement that manifested itself in the Public Sector was sparked and developed apart from political parties, and this suspension of partisanship, almost inconceivable in the society of the time—and above all among the Jews, who are especially prone to it—typifies the ghetto's social institutions, unique among their kind, with distinctive features determined by the exceptional circumstances that had given rise to them.

VII. THE GHETTO'S POLITICAL PARTIES, THE INDEPENDENT SOCIAL MOVEMENT, AND THE *JUDENRAT'S* ATTITUDE TOWARD THEM

In the era my memoirs cover (from November 1940 to September 1942), community work was not carried on around political parties. The latter obviously continued to exist in the ghetto, but mainly as a small number of central organs; their representatives made up an advisory committee for the AJDC. The Joint Distribution Committee, above all through its two directors Giterman and Guzik, never ceased to play an important role in ghetto life, even if the general political situation often forced it to alter the forms of its activity. The AJDC likewise provided the parties with the funds necessary for their ranks to exist. They ran some of the people's kitchens. The committee directing Mutual Aid was mostly composed of representatives of these groups, in line with the AJDC's tenets. But despite the various guises political parties assumed, I can attest, through my continued contact with people, that the parties had not made deep inroads in this period into the bulk of the population. It isn't hard to understand why. Among other reasons there was the need for secrecy, which had to be strengthened further after many community workers were murdered in April 1942. And, above all else, the activity of political parties requires the existence of a regime liberal enough to give them the chance to influence politics through public opinion. But in the prevailing breakdown of social classes, in a society stripped of organic economic structure and living under a continual external threat, what place was there for political work?

In the case of the Zionist parties, emigration propaganda, as well as fund-raising for it, obviously became pointless. Even so, from what we can judge, of all the political groups, those of the left-wing Zionist youth were the most numerous.

As for the socialist groups, how could they organize the struggle to improve the living conditions of the working class, at a time when every worker was ready to accept any working condition at all, just to be let into the workshops that gave him the illusion he could save himself and his family from the onrush of exterminations?

I recall attending a meeting convened by Doctor Ringelblum, who was determined to improve the fate of workers hired by Jewish subcontractors for German firms. The motion was made to attempt to influence these entrepreneurs; but unfortunately, this noble initiative was fruitless, since social problems of this sort cannot be resolved by "reasoning with" starving people—and in this period we could have no other battle strategy.

This activity, outside political parties, on the part of all the institutions in the Public Sector was something so unusual that the party committees did not initially recognize its real value, treating it with a certain amount of genuine distrust. For this reason we were generally not invited to the meetings held at Mutual Aid, which party representatives did attend. In the winter of 1941–42, however, we were invited to one of these meetings. I attended as president of the Central Commission of Tenement Committees, accompanied by another member of our office—Izaia Rabinovitch. In his political persuasion this man, a well-to-do merchant from an Orthodox family, was a staunch *Bundist*. Sincerity, moral integrity, and devotion to social work—these were the characteristic traits that earned him the respect and veneration of all who had dealings with him. Both of us took an active part in the debates. When the meeting was over, the leader of the leftist faction of the *Poalei-Zion* group, Szachne Sagan, said to me, with that touch of humor that never deserted him: "Well, you're not as frightened as we thought you'd be. But we were still pretty scared of you."

The *Judenrat* would periodically try to seize control of the independent social institutions. It first went after the broad network of Tenement Committees, but it realized how hard it would be to forcibly subjugate an administrative apparatus made up of volunteer workers; if need be, the committees would simply rather have ceased their work. This is why, when it met with resistance, the *Judenrat* invariably deferred its plans. But one of these efforts, made in the spring of 1942, was more categorical, and as usual the *Judenrat* offered its favorite blackmailing argument—German demands. To register a protest with the president of the *Judenrat*, a delegation was organized, made up of representatives of all parties. I too was asked to take part. The delegate from the *Bund*, Moritz Orzech, who had come to negotiate with me about this issue, framed his proposal this way: "We will be participating as representatives of public opinion, and you as representatives of new forces that have arisen in the ghetto."

With the assent of the executive board of our Central Commission, I joined the delegation, which also included— as I quite vividly remember—for the General Zionists, Menachem Kirszenbaum; for the leftist faction of the *Poalei-Zion*, Szachne Sagan; for the *Bund*, Maurycy Orzech;

and for the *Agudah*, Zisze Frydman. Also, if I'm not mistaken, we were joined by: Sak, from the conservative faction of the *Poalei-Zion*, and Salomon Mazur for the *Mizrahi.**

Led for this solemn audience into the office of President Czerniakow, we demanded, one after the other, that the independence of the social institutions be safeguarded, emphasizing that we would consider any infringement upon our autonomy as an act of violence, for which he would in future bear the full weight of responsibility . . . . Unfortunately, for all the threatening signs about us, we did not at that moment see that the people of the ghetto had no future to bargain over.

Since the *Judenrat* was particularly violating the rights of the new forces I represented, it was my duty, while insisting on safeguards for our independence, to stress at the same time how important the involvement of my comrades was; and I told the president that although they were now being thoroughly hampered in their activity, these workers represented every stripe of public opinion and all the ideological and dynamic forces that would guide the whole of Judaism after the liberation.

The next day Giterman informed me that the members of the delegation approved the viewpoint I'd presented, and the formula "ideological and dynamic forces" spread among the ghetto's social-activist circles.

The stance we took with the president of the *Judenrat* brought good results: once more, the "categorical demands of the Germans" were forgotten, and the social service institutions continued to exist as before.

---

* Political parties among the Jews of pre-war Poland were numerous. Briefly, the *Bund* was a non-Zionist socialist party; the *Agudah*, a religious party; the *Mizrahi*, a religious Zionist party, and the *Poalei-Zion*, a socialist Zionist party. [Translator's note.]

This visit to the president was marked by the following episode: The door was abruptly flung open, and the room was invaded by six Germans in uniform. The head of the group declared this was a visit from a general of the Reich police, and the entire group advanced in regular step, without stopping, toward the president's table. He signalled for us to wait in the next room. When he had us brought back in, a half hour later, the Germans had already left his office.

Half in jest one day, I swore I would never cross the threshold of the *Judenrat* unless I was forced to, but this was in fact the only time I had broken my oath. I wanted to use our visit, then, to get a sense of the general atmosphere there. Walking through the corridors, I noticed a group of people to whom a young policeman was making excited gestures as he told a story. I approached them with Mr. Orzech, who knew this young man, who repeated his story for us. The inauguration (or some other celebration) for a children's center was to take place that day in a square not far from the *Judenrat*. He had noticed, in passing, that his colleague, who was on duty, was not letting in poorly dressed children. His protests were futile, because his colleague insisted he was following orders. Indignant, the young policeman went to complain to the vice-president of the *Judenrat*, the engineer Lichtenbaum, and was given a sharp reprimand for meddling in matters that were none of his concern.

Continuing on my way I witnessed another fairly characteristic scene, insignificant though it might seem. A *Judenrat* employee was making a call from a telephone in the corridor. The door right by the phone opened, a secretary rushed up to him and ordered him to hang up immediately, because the head of service, a Mr. A., needed the line. This Mr. A. was the *Judenrat*'s head of labor services; that is, the service that provided the Germans with manpower for forced labor. The employee tried to explain that it was an urgent call, but, at the secretary's urging, he was forced to hang up anyway and handed the receiver to the service head, who appeared right at that moment.

These episodes reflect, as though in a distorting mirror, some characteristic features that had developed in certain Polish-Jewish milieux.

If before 1935–36 anti-semitism in Poland did not assume brutal guises, it nevertheless had a recognizable character. It permeated all levels of Polish society, and it was simply viewed as good form to complain that "the Jews had invaded Poland." In their relations with the Poles, the Jews felt surrounded by an air of mistrust, ill-will, and deliberate isolation. As a result of this treatment, an inferiority complex developed among them, especially among the young who had attended Polish schools. Attempts to repress or combat this complex often turned into a kind of affected bravado, which in certain individuals degenerated into what we call *chutzpah*. This inferiority complex was further amplified by the fact that, with only a few exceptions, the Jews were barred from performing any civil function. Jews did of course occupy high positions in commerce and industry as well as in the liberal professions, but access to all posts in government or in public institutions, whose exercise entails day-to-day contact with large masses of the population, was forbidden them. In Poland there was not a single Jewish policeman or bailiff, and even such posts as concierge, postman, or trolley conductor were reserved for non-Jews.

The resulting psychic repression naturally sought some outlet, and the compensation the high officials of the ghetto were offered took a repulsive, grotesque form. Thus, the gentlemen of the *Judenrat* demanded a slavish obedience to the authorities, and cultivated a certain grandiose style among their circle, while the Jewish police underscored the hierarchical differences in its own ranks and displayed its authority by mistreating the ghetto's poorer residents.

In this regard I cannot forget a little scene that took place in the winter of 1940–41 on Ciepla Street, which was furrowed with cracks after the 1939 bombings, and, at the time of my story, heaped with snow. An old, malnourished Jew, in rags, was pulling a heavily laden handcart. Unable to steer its weight on such a bumpy path, he could no longer pull it, and the cart rolled onto the sidewalk. The Jewish policeman, posted nearby, could not tolerate such an offense, and dealt this wretched man a violent blow on the back with his club. Asserting all the prerogatives of his authority, he vehemently countered the protests of passersby.

Yet most people in the ghetto always rose up against the abuses of the Jewish police and took the side of those they had mistreated. Conflicts with the police over such episodes were a daily occurrence, and one incident even ended in tragedy. In defending a woman who had been beaten black and blue by a policeman at the corner of Zelazna Street, a doctor (whose name escapes me) became so emotional that he suffered a heart attack. After a violent quarrel with one police dignitary the *Bund* leader, Mr. Orzech, was arrested for several days by the *Judenrat*.

Both before the war and in the ghetto I had occasion to observe many manifestations of the psychic deformity I've described, but within the confines of the present work I could only present it in a simplistic form. This is why my statement—incidentally, like all generalizations about collective states of mind—is subject to certain qualifications.

Thus, the process of psychic deformation had little hold over most of the Jews in Poland, who were quite orthodox, kept up the ancient traditions and medieval garb, and in effect lived in a kind of ghetto, having almost no dealings with the Polish population. Moreover, the two large public movements—Zionism and socialism—reinforced the Jews' sense of their dignity and kept them from succumbing to an inferiority complex and the warping it produced.

The strata of Jewish society most contaminated by this pathology were the small-time tradesmen, business clerks, and, above all, liberal professionals. As a general rule the more antisemitic the social circles with which the Jews associated were, the more urgently they felt the subconscious need to repress and compensate for their inferiority complex. In Poland, the legal profession cultivated the most thoroughgoing antisemitism; in the years just prior to the war, it assumed a positively Hitlerian stamp, and it was precisely the young generation of Jewish lawyers who bore the most marked symptoms of warped psyches. Their active participation in the ghetto's Jewish police force was not unrelated to this.

As I continued down the corridor toward the room where the other members of the delegations were awaiting me, I met an old friend of mine, the engineer Michal Krol, secretary general of the *Judenrat*. We had not met since the occupation began, and were very happy to see each another again. Krul was a man of noble character, profound, serene, and his life had taken quite an uncommon turn. In his youth, he had been active in the revolutionary movement in Poland. In 1905, the Russian czarist government had sentenced him to forced labor, and he was deported to Siberia, from which he returned only in 1918. His fiancée had waited for him all those years, and as soon as he returned they wed. Yet his happiness was to be short-lived: his wife died in childbirth and the child did not survive. Ever since then Krul remained on his own. In the course of his revolutionary activity he was a comrade to all the men who later occupied the highest posts in the Polish government; he had shared a prison cell in Siberia with one of the secretary-presidents. In a word, he had what are called "influential relations." Only, insofar as these men had abandoned the path of democracy and allied themselves with the totalitarian, anti-semitic regime, he grew further and further estranged from them. He was without a trace of pretension or ambition, and I was startled to learn he had accepted a post in the *Judenrat*. We went into his office and sat facing each other. Looking at me with his deep, sad eyes, he answered the question I could not bring myself to raise: "Here or elsewhere—isn't it all the same? Maybe here it's still possible to do something." His voice lacked conviction, I felt his immense moral weariness. It was our last encounter. Soon after, exanthematic typhus claimed him.

VIII. THE CREATION OF THE GHETTO

No sooner was Warsaw occupied than rumors based on certain indications started to circulate, according to which Jews would be forbidden to remain at their addresses. For the first few days, before anyone had time to seize our wireless sets, a broadcast from London announced to us that the Germans intended to transfer all the Jews in Poland to the eastern part of the Lublin region. Another source confirmed this news for us: friends living in this region informed me that, in private conversations, certain Germans had told them that they would be remaining where they were, while the Jews of other regions would be joining them.

The first rumors about the ghetto go back to October 1939, and various data would suggest that the planning of a Warsaw ghetto was already the order of the day among the Germans, although it first appeared inachievable. For the time being they abandoned the plan. Shortly after, however, walls sealing off the streets were erected. Sometimes these walls were demolished and transported to some other area, to reduce the space they were supposed to encircle. Optimists assumed these walls were strategic in character, but little by little it became obvious these measures were the prelude to the creation of the ghetto. The Jews lived in a state of constant nervous strain and uncertainty. Torture "by uncertainty" was by no means a chance effect, but an integral part of the German system. Around June 1940, the Jews were forbidden to move into certain districts of the city, and immediately thereafter, the expulsions of Jews from whole apartment blocks began in these districts. News of the expulsions reached us every day. If you met acquaintances, the first question you put to them was whether they still lived in their own apartment. The expulsions were carried out in the following manner: the Germans would surround an entire block, which the Jews had to vacate within half an hour, taking with them only personal effects. Sometimes, the vacated premises would remain unoccupied for some time, and the Jews managed to steal some portion of their own furniture from their apartments. My wife and I were expelled in this fashion at the start of August 1940, at 10:00 A.M. The German soldiers assigned to the apartment arrived toward evening, when the building was already to have been cleared of Jews—made *judenrein*. My wife was still there, however, and they told her: "Take what you want. We haven't seen a thing." The German soldiers took our furniture down and loaded it onto a truck. This is how, having rented a room on Senatorska Street, we managed to transport part of our furniture and my library. Our landlady, Mme B., was a highly cultivated woman, a doctor who taught at the university; she had done her studies in France and owned a library of French authors and many mementos of Paris. As the apartment was Aryan, the Germans would not venture there. After being subjected, in our former dwelling, to numerous visits from German officials and German looters, too, this new refuge gave us a certain sense of relaxation and the illusion of safety.

But here I have to recount an episode that dates to this period. I happened to be on Senatorska Street, near No. 30, right by my own building. Two men in civilian clothing rushed up to me, grabbed me by the arm, and, without saying a word, dragged me into the courtyard. Without quite realizing what was happening, I tried to resist and break free of them. Whereupon the enemy immediately received reinforcements. Lashes of a riding crop were raining down on my head, my glasses shattered, my face was bloodied. I heard the shouts: *"Jude, arbeiten!"* ("Get to work, Jew!") It was a group of Polish workers led by a German (the man with the riding crop), and they were removing equipment from a Jewish printing house. I had no choice but to submit and load two or three cases onto a truck. At a certain moment, an old Polish worker signaled to me to clear off, which I did without delay. By this point we were hardened and inured to unforeseen troubles. I was due to speak in an hour at a meeting in the suburb of Mokotow, at the other end of town. I had just enough time to wash the blood stains off my face; I showed up at the meeting at the appointed hour.

Senatorska Street at that time was not yet off limits to Jews, and we hoped to be able to remain there. But when the borders of the ghetto were laid out some weeks later, this street was not included, and we had to move once again. We set out in search of a room and spent whole days going from one house to another, only to come back in the evening empty-handed. Luckily, in the course of this search, my wife managed to find a room at 32 Elektoralna Street, with the family of a doctor we knew. We had planned, for greater security, to leave our furniture and library with our former landlady, but as the moving day approached, we noticed signs of great agitation on her part, and one day a truck stopped in front of the building, onto which she had the best pieces of her own furnishings loaded. We learned then that, according to the racial laws, she was considered a Jewess and would also have to go into the ghetto. Once there, she continued to practice medicine, and my wife hired her for medical assistance at the Refugee Center at 12 Elektoralna Street.

Once the borders of the ghetto were established, and for the entire period allotted for the transfer of the Jews, there was no limit to the shifts that took place. As blocks of tenements and whole streets were closed off, Aryan houses were sometimes added by way of a tradeoff. Consequently, some Jews had to change residence several times. Even after this period, changes in the ghetto borders continued to occur; its territory was systematically delimited, and rumors started flying that the "little ghetto" would be totally liquidated. Like hunted animals, the ghetto inhabitants made a dash for some shelter or lodging, which became harder and harder to find. All this created an atmosphere of helpless confusion among the Jews, whose nerves had already been put to extreme tests—but that, after all, was the aim of the Germans' psychological treatment: the Jews were to be kept in a state of depression that would render them incapable of any resistance at the moment the Final Solution would be achieved.

The posters announcing the creation of the ghetto were put up on the eve of *Yom Kippur,* on October 16, 1940; on November 15 the ghetto's gates were shut, presenting to the world an hitherto unimagined example of human cohabitation. During this brief period, all the Jews living outside the ghetto, around 140,000 in number, were to be integrated into it. The city took on the unaccustomed aspect of a vast nomad camp, traversed by thousands of handcarts pushed by entire families—children as well as old people. So were the Jews driven out of their homes into the uncertainty of the ghetto.

What were their feelings then? To answer this question, I must join introspection to observation. The ghetto, whose terrifying image started looming before us from the first days of the occupation, still seemed like some unimaginable nightmare; yet just one year of daily torments under the German rod had sufficed to blunt our sensitivity. In our apartments we were never safe, having to put up with the official, semiofficial, and plainly thieving visits of the Germans, often acompanied by beatings and violence, against which we were powerless to struggle. From November 12, 1939, when it became mandatory to wear the Jewish armband, every venture out of one's house became a torture. In the streets, they hunted Jews, making them do chores that were for the most part absurd and humiliating. The malevolent, sometimes openly hostile attitude of the Polish population only heightened the bitterness. The longing to go and hide somewhere, in order not to be seen and to see no one, occasionally deluded us into supposing that the ghetto would shield us from this hate-filled world. The immense fatigue that came out of the difficulties of finding a roof in the ghetto, the deep, essential feeling of the absurdity of all that was happening, and at the same time of its ineluctability, had done their work, and the exodus into the ghetto was tinged with a mute, bustling austerity.

The most painful situation was that of the destitute Jews who filled the suburb of Praga. Without any means, they had the hardest time finding a nook for themselves in the ghetto; and it was in this quarter that the Polish police showed excessive zeal, hunting the poor wretches out of their homes before the scheduled date. In general, though, the transfer went calmly, without the grave casualties we had feared. The Poles were so surprised by the way the exodus of the Jews took place that they did not even show them malice—not that this kept them, by the way, from taking instant possession of their inheritance. At the very start of the occupation we had sublet a room from a couple of civil servants. When, in August 1940, we were driven out of our apartment and wanted to take along an armchair that was in their room, our heirs voiced categorical opposition to this reduction in their inheritance portion. The oft-heard wish of the prewar years, that the Jews should leave for Madagascar as wretched as the tramps they were when they came to Poland, had prepared the Polish mentality to assimilate German methods, a fact the Germans anticipated all too well.

IX. COMMUNITY WORK IN THE GHETTO:
PORTRAITS OF COMMUNITY WORKERS

While the exodus into the ghetto was under way, communi-ty work escalated to a pitch that left our district of Mutual Aid not a moment's rest—which, luckily, kept us from thinking about our own fate. Our part of town was among the wealthiest, but recent days had revealed just how much Jewish misery it was harboring: whole throngs now flooded the district in search of some form of subsidy, be it to find means for moving their furniture, or to leave deposits for the wretched abodes they would rent in the ghetto. The sums we had available were inadequate, and, in order to come up with additional allocations, I had to circulate several times a day between my district and the Central Office of Mutual Aid, housed at the Judaic Institute on Tlomacka Street.

The help provided while the Jews were being transferred into the ghetto was the last manifestation of the activity of Mutual Aid's eighth district. Since there were no Jews left in this part of the city, this district, as well as that of the suburb of Praga, on the right bank of the Vistula, were eliminated. On the territory that roughly corresponded to the site of the ghetto, there remained five districts of Mutual Aid, but a sixth was formed for the section of the ghetto that contained the densest and poorest population. This district was set up at 29 Nowolipki Street, a part of which lay within its borders (between Karmelicka and Smocza Streets), as did a part of Dzielna, Pawia, Gesia, Smocza, Mila and finally Lubeckiego, Ostrowska, and Niska Streets, the last three of which were inhabited by the very poorest Jews.

How can I possibly convey to my readers the feelings that surface as I name all these streets? Over some two years spent in this district, I constantly surveyed the wretched life of the people who teemed in its streets, now driven to despair, now clinging to the illusion of an uncertain, highly improbable hope. All this life, the thoughts and sentiments of these human beings, were destroyed, snuffed out like vermin, without a trace, as though they had never existed. Even the streets disappeared, not a house remained standing, nothing but heaps of rubble in what was then a bustling quarter. But when the ghetto came into existence, we could not foresee this terrible ontological emptiness. For us, that quarter was full of living human beings reduced to dire poverty; they needed help to struggle for their right to stay alive, to go on believing in the future, which would allow them, as in the past, to derive the meaning of life from this eternal source of man's meager happiness.

The former three districts were dissolved, and the administration of the newly created sixth district was formed anew. But in recognizing the fact that our earlier Commission of Instruction and Inspection was a unitary body, coordinated and experienced, our whole team, in keeping with my agreement with Dr. Ringelblum, was expected to fulfill the same functions in the new sixth district and remained in its place until the sudden disaster of July 1942. This would be an apt place, incidentally, to mention my most active collaborator, Jozef Krakowski, with whom I worked in perfect harmony until his death (from exanthematic typhus, in the winter of 1941–42).

Our new district comprised more than 100,000 inhabitants and some 250 buildings. For each of the latter we had, of course, to set up a corresponding number of Tenement Committees. The district included a high percentage of newlyarrived families, that is to say, families without means, with no source of income, and as yet unadapted to their new living conditions. The dire poverty, overcrowding, and chaos were indescribable. It was clearly impossible for Mutual Aid to govern the situation, which heightened the need for the immediate help that did come directly from person to person, through the intervention of the Tenement Committees.

Now that we had started to visit the tenement inhabitants, we saw with our own eyes what the ghetto apartments really were. They were hovels, overcrowded in the extreme, true hotbeds of famine and sickness. The visitors' reports our comrades would turn in to the commission were tinged with despair, the vision of the City of Death would loom up before our eyes, and it took the greatest effort to organize work amid this raging chaos of human misery. For our commission, whose sphere of activity was the richest section of the city, the difference between the problems we now had to solve and the working conditions of former times was striking. The Jewish population of our former district had mostly been composed of merchants and members of the professions. These had also been the milieux in which the members of the Tenement Committees were recruited, whereas here we were faced with the masses of petty merchants, craftsmen, and workers—lives in social disintegration and moral disorientation. It was clear through our observations that the multitude of new arrivals had disorganized the Tenement Committees' activities. It was necessary to reorganize them, to integrate the new elements into them and get them to participate in work that had in any event to be stepped up. After careful reflection we decided that the only way of succeeding was to reelect all the Tenement Committees in the district. But accomplishing this task took a huge preliminary effort: assessing the situation in each apartment building, coming to an agreement with the existing committee, calling a general meeting of tenants, and sending our instructors to each meeting.

Carrying out this vast project obviously exceeded the possibilities our commission could present with its only seven or eight members. We therefore set about recruiting volunteer social assistants, and this team quickly rose to forty willing and able people, each taking responsibility for five to six buildings. Eventually some of them left us, some by despair, others due to the famine, but a group of around twenty kept their positions to the bitter end; new volunteers took the place of those who had left, and thus the activities of the social assistants extended over the entire district and went on uninterruptedly.

In the other districts, the number of community relief workers was lower, and, from an organizational standpoint, they belonged to the Commission of Instruction and Inspection.

The working conditions for the community volunteers were extremely difficult: the masses with whom they worked were in a state of disorder and confusion. Hunger, typhus, and dysentery were felling these people, who wanted eagerly to serve their even less fortunate brothers. But in these conditions, continual orientation and inspection were necessary to bring these generous impulses to maximum efficiency. The meetings devoted to orientation and elections took place evenings in apartment buildings, after curfew; also, the community worker taking part in the meeting had to stay overnight in that building; most often he would spend the night in a chair, in the corner of an overcrowded room. In this way, certain workers contracted typhus, some succumbed to it, and all the others without exception perished in the course of total extermination. After the end of the war, I met one of them who had escaped the massacre. But as the conditions our work took place in grew more complicated, we closed our ranks, and our commission and the team of our community assistants had become a sort of brotherhoood. The intensity of the work, the gravity of the problems we had to confront, the contact with the masses—all this totally absorbed us, without leaving us the leisure to reflect on what awaited us, and gave deep meaning to our life.

Despite their individual differences, the people in this team were united by the awareness that, since they were caught up in highly tragic events, they had to face them, without giving way to any secondary, petty considerations. An air of implacable austerity emanated from them, yet at the same time they radiated understanding and humanity. In the central administration of Mutual Aid, they were more respected than liked; when the directors of Mutual Aid learned through our reports that people had criticisms about them, they requested that I allow their delegate to attend our next meeting to offer explanations.

Considering that all these people were unpaid workers, and many of them were themselves in real hardship and forever going hungry, the existence of such a united, dynamic team seems a miracle.

One of these community assistants, Isaac Notes, springs to mind. He had lived all winter with his sister in an unheated room the door of which had been broken down. They never undressed. Eventually his sister contracted pneumonia and died, but he himself, hungry and filthy, continued his labors indefatigably in the poorest houses. In all our meetings he lashed out at the laziness, indifference, and iniquity of official welfare services, including Mutual Aid; his criticisms were caustic and severe, on occasion exaggerated, yet his words bespoke such compassion for human misery that it was impossible not to pay heed to them.

Everyone considered Jewish according to the racial laws, including a fairly high number of converts who had sealed their break with Judaism by baptism, were sent into the ghetto. In Poland, where anti-semitism pervaded every sector of society, a Jew who underwent baptism was above all performing a social (and not a religious) rite, which meant to cut all ties with Judaism. In the ghetto, a good many of the converts kept aloof, trying to play the role of an elite. The Catholic charity organization *Caritas* operated on their behalf, and the ghetto had two Catholic churches, always full of worshippers, for their use. The sight of this crowd wearing Jewish armbands while fervently praying in a Catholic church created a strange impression.

There also existed in the ghetto a large number of Jews who had converted after the outbreak of the war, hoping in this way to avoid their people's impending fate. And, in fact, rumors circulated that the Catholic clergy was interceding for them, would authorize their leaving the ghetto, etc. All such hopes were in vain: the Catholic Jews shared the fate of those they wanted to disown as brethren. At the start of the

Große Aktion, among the first victims were the workers in the workshop organized by *Caritas*, and their families.

The ghetto contained assimilated Jews who were completely distanced from Judaism by their education and mentality. This assimilation was a typical tendency for a part of Polish Jewry; nevertheless, this group also contained a certain number of members of the true intellectual elite. One of its most eminent representatives was the lawyer Leon Berenson, who had litigated in the great political trials of the czarist era and who was the first diplomatic representative of Poland to the Ukraine. In the ghetto Berenson made it his mission to work in the area of social welfare. I had met him several times at the Center for Mutual Aid, where he initiated himself into the work, but he admitted to me one day that it was hard for him to adapt to the methods and atmosphere prevailing there. I invited him to come to one of the meetings of our community assistants. This meeting took place on a cold, damp winter day, in an unheated room. We were seated, muffled in our coats; our breath made a thick mist, so that each of us looked like a steam engine going at full speed. This was one of our regular meetings, with reports presented on the situation in tenements and discussion of current issues, with animated criticism and protest. All this went on in our usual atmosphere of stark sincerity and blunt candor. And Berenson, a stranger in our midst, understood, by virtue of his intellectual experience, that authentic human values had been safeguarded there. He expressed a desire to come back, to keep contact with us, but his intentions were not to be furthered: he died shortly after from a heart ailment, without having figured—and how lucky for him—among the martyrs of Treblinka.

Our volunteers kept their course in the sea of woes that surrounded them. One can unhesitatingly apply to them the words of the Russian poet:

Without knowledge of sadness or anger
No one can love his country.

They would not tone down their bitter words, their demands were often impossible to satisfy, and their criticisms pitiless— and in these moments of vented rage, the person best suited to calm them down was an exceptional woman who worked among us and was the soul of our team. Czeslawa Raifeld-Pechnik was a woman of thirty, who, by her radiant sincerity and beauty, had the gift to move the hearts of those about her. In the course of a collection, she was assigned to a building we expected to contribute three hundred zlotys; after her speech, we took in three thousand. When a despairing crowd of refugees or recent expulsions besieged the district, she would mingle with this vermin-infested multitude, taking children into her arms, summoning a word of consolation for everyone. The warnings we made to her were unavailing; this admirable woman would answer: "Under the present conditions, to die of typhus transmitted by a louse isn't the worst of deaths." Having used up all her private means, she was obliged to accept paid employment, but the bureaucratic routine stifled the sacred fire that animated her, and this was a source of anguish for her. She saw things more clearly than the others. At a time when the idea had never crossed our minds, she said that we would all be deported and exterminated, and when her sinister premonitions began to come true, she refused to get exemption papers for herself, not wanting to survive her mother, if the latter should perish. Around August 15, 1942, she was deported to Treblinka with her entire family.

In our milieu, there were people of all ages—young people as well as old—from all professions, from workers to intellectuals, and of every political stripe, from revisionists to all varieties of socialists. In this limited sector, the extra-political character of our organization's activity was again affirmed. It is also interesting to note, without drawing definite conclusions about it, that all our relief workers belonged to secular parties; community welfare assistants, at least (and not the members of the Tenement Committees either), did not include the *Mizrahis* and *Agudists*.

Since fate put me at the head of this altogether unique team I have the obligation, by virtue of various memories I retain, of preserving my valiant colleagues from oblivion. Alas! I have forgotten certain names and certain faces, the images of some of them return to me shrouded in mist, fading immediately, and there are few whom I can remember precisely.

I see Frenkel, jack-of-all-trades, sixty-five years old. Neglecting his business, he devoted all his time to the tenements assigned to him. One day he fell ill and his elderly wife came to me for advice. She said to me: "I do a little business, but my husband has to work for those who are suffering; that's how it has to be for the present." At the start of the *Große Aktion* this woman rushed up to me, beside herself with despair: her husband had been taken. I managed to come up with exemption papers through Wielikowski, and Frenkel was released. Unfortunately not for long, though: a few days later, he was taken off again, with his wife, this time for good.

I also remember the revisionist Kirschenberg, a young man exuding energy and optimism, and a group of three members of the *Bund* with whom I had strong ties. One of them was Schwarzberg, a young worker with an open expression, always smiling. To subsist, he accepted backbreaking physical labor, which he performed with great ease and good humor, without, however, interrupting his activity as an instructor in the tenement houses of his sector.

The second *Bund* member was Goldheimer, a man with delicate features and melancholic eyes, radiating goodness. Before the war he had been a traveling salesman, and earned a good living. In the ghetto his material situation was quite tenuous; he literally shrank before our eyes, yet all his attention was focused on the suffering of others. Every Saturday, at the end of the morning, I would organize meetings with our community aides. Goldheimer never missed them. I discovered, however, that, once a week at this very time, he had the opportunity to eat his fill, since he was invited to lunch every Saturday at a friend's. My insistence to him that he go for that lunch instead of coming to the meeting couldn't sway him, and I had to change the hour of our meetings.

The third and most remarkable member of this group was Zanwel Dywan, a true representative of the intelligentsia. For some consecutive years he had been the leader of the *Bund* chapter in the town council of Plock. He had lived for a long time in England, from which he had brought back a library of English authors. In the ghetto, he maintained himself by giving English lessons, though the number of his students dwindled, and his situation grew more and more calamitous. One day, passing an outdoor secondhand book dealer, I chanced upon volumes of Macaulay's *History of England* bearing his intitials, and realized the degree of misery to which he had sunk, to be forced to part with his library books. His sensitivity to human suffering and injustice was extraordinary. I recall the reports he would give at our meetings about the poverty and misfortune he had observed in the buildings of his sector; his voice never betrayed anger, but was tinged with a deeply felt sorrow.

Exceptionally, the community assistants of the sixth district were entitled to a representative in the Central Commission of Tenement Committees; they chose Dywan, a man of such integrity that he could not get his bearings in the complicated machinery of the ghetto's social institutions. The idealism that pervaded his speeches at times had a utopian cast to it, his plans were often unfeasible, yet his whole person emanated such humanity and nobility of thought that we called him "the conscience of the Central Commission."

The reader may raise the perfectly justified question: How could the social welfare organization tolerate such misery among its most active and devoted colleagues? The explanation resides in the altogether special conditions that prevailed in this city of death that was the Warsaw ghetto, conditions no language can convey. In particular, the Public Sector had no funds of its own: our work consisted of setting up the Tenement Committees and overseeing the welfare aid directly contributed in the building from person to person. The only thing we managed to create in this area was a fund for individual help, sustained by the modest sums drawn from collections in the Tenement Committees. These amounts were plainly inadequate: in allocating them for needy men within the elite, we could give each a tiny one-time sum every few months. Occasionally it was possible for us to secure our assistants free coupons for the soup irregularly distributed by the people's kitchens, but that was also not enough to keep a human being from going hungry. Such was the fate of this doomed, hermetically sealed world, a fate which thrust helpers and helped alike into a giant common grave.

X. THE ACTIVITY OF THE TENEMENT COMMITTEES
AND THEIR CENTRAL COMMISSION

As far as I know, no publication about the Warsaw ghetto has included the history of its highly unique social institutions, even in the fragmentary form I have presented in the preceding chapters.

In my efforts to convey some idea of these institutions, which were the spontaneous manifestation of the humanism and solidarity of the masses, I was reduced to recounting only a few elements still in my memory, for in Paris, where I am writing, I have no documents. Yet even in the time of the ghetto we realized that the life we were leading in it, and above all our social institutions, would be of some interest to future generations. The archives Dr. Ringelblum assembled were the essential proof of this notion. For our part, in the Public Sector we tried to preserve traces of our work in accounts of the activity of all these institutions. Even for the core cell—the Tenement Committee—a unique form of report was devised taking stock of all phases of its activity: collection and distribution of funds as well as all other forms of aid. Numerous tenement committees regularly wrote up minutes of their meetings, with copies handed over to the Mutual Aid center. As for the Central Commission of Tenement Committees, since the main issues were debated there, its minutes were veritable shorthand texts. Our highly competent secretary, Sara Polus, executed them with a precision that would have qualified her for work in any parliament. Every meeting began with my report on the general situation of the previous week, followed by an exchange of opinions. Next, the proceedings entertained any questions in the area of social welfare which had to be resolved or reformed. Representatives of Mutual Aid and of the *KOM* were often invited to take part in our meetings. The minutes were recorded in twenty copies and sent off to the districts, to the other social institutions, and to Dr. Ringelblum. These minutes would prove of inestimable value in explaining the workings of ghetto life, and there is every certainty that Dr. Ringelblum kept them in his archives. A part of these archives disappeared and was found only recently, most of them managed to be saved and are housed today in Poland's Jewish Historical Institute. Unfortunately, my efforts to obtain from this institute copies of the minutes, or at least the confirmation that they exist, have been in vain. Thus, these documents, as well as certain others whose existence is indisputable, are unavailable to me, and the only source of my writings has been my memory. This circumstance has induced me, rather than to narrate the material systematically, to limit myself to recounting isolated episodes that to some extent reflect the activity of relief organizations in the ghetto. I therefore will attempt, on the basis of my recollections, to conjure up, however summarily, the essential characteristics of these organizations.

The basic cell of the Public Sector—the elected committee in each apartment building—gradually changed the form of its activity. The course of its evolution was as follows: in its original conception, the Tenement Committee was to be the local organ of the Central Institution for Mutual Aid and subject to its guidelines. All funds gathered were to be turned over to the Center, whose duty it was to redistribute them among the Tenement Committees for local needs. The principle was sound in theory, because it tended toward an equitable distribution of aid, regardless of the population size and the wealth of each building. Yet this cogent system collapsed under real-life demands. As time wore on, misery increased; certain tenements were populated only by the poor, and even the apartment buildings considered well-off contained such a large number of needy people that it was not possible to cover their most basic needs. Obviously the committee and the residents of each building were best qualified to judge their specific miseries, and obviously, in these conditions, it was hard to have the funds turned over for centralized, institution-led distribution. Every committee tried by every means possible to help the needy of its own building. This form of activity roused the committee's energy, while giving it a humanitarian character; for direct, person-to-person help had a concrete, tangible form: every donor could see with his own eyes the results of his good deed. But on the other hand, this autonomous activity of the Tenement Committees called for increased effort on our part in orientating and supervising them. From the first months of the ghetto's existence, we had to recognize this evolution as a given, and the Tenement Committees, which at the outset were only groups for collecting and distributing Mutual Aid, were transformed into autonomous organs of local relief.

Mutual Aid (its official administrative apparatus) limited itself to demanding a certain allotment of funds on its behalf. This issue did not fall within the domain of our group of volunteers, but rather in that of the finance administrators of the Sector. The Tenement Committees were always in opposition to this and generally gave Mutual Aid only a very small percentage of their collections. With this money, the Center for Mutual Aid had created a fund for individual relief, whose distribution was in the hands of the administrative apparatus of Dr. Ringelblum and the Central Commission of Tenement Committees (the latter represented at meetings by myself or a delegate of mine). I recall the tragic atmosphere of these meetings: we were deluged with requests; each case demonstrated the petitioner's extreme need and at times hopeless predicament. And there we were, impotent before such an ocean of human sufferings! Should we divide the available funds into equal parts among all the applicants? If we did, the assistance would have no effect whatsoever: it would not be enough to buy a kilo of bread for each person. On the other hand, if we made a selection, whom should we choose? How could we possibly decide to grant one person even temporary help, while refusing someone else? Forced by circumstance to sift through requests, we ended up granting subsidies either to people of particular merit in their record of social activity, or to particularly urgent cases: thus, aid was granted to improve the nutrition of people who had withstood exanthematic typhus.

But in general, and in this area as well, we continually faced a problem that, like any other vital problem of the ghetto, could admit of no solution in this City of Death. Due to the conditions explained above, individual aid from the Center was really insignificant; the importance of the Public Sector consisted of the direct actions of the Tenement Committees. These groups jealously guarded their autonomy. I often heard their representatives say: "We're little 'Joint Committees,' each building needs its little 'Joint Committee' right now."

For our part, we tended to give these small "joint distribution committees" the form of organized institutions and to assign tasks to their members. At a general meeting, each apartment house conducted elections for the president, secretary, treasurer, reporters on matters of food supplies, clothing, children's aid, a commission to create profit-making ventures, patronage for refugee centers, etc.

Eventually conflicts arose within the committees, which sometimes, especially in our district, grew quite sharp. To resolve them, a court of arbitration was set up, functioning along the judicial guidelines we laid out. The actual subjects of conflict have slipped my mind, but I do remember well the prevailing atmosphere of these court sessions. The parties often showed up in a state of great agitation, ready to strike at each other, but as debates opened up and the interested sides, one after the other and in strict order of precedence, were allowed to express their grievances in full, the dark mood began to lift, the frenzy died down, and generally some arrangement was reached without the tribunal having to give a ruling.

This arbitration court, and all other organs of the Sector, had, in addition to their direct tasks, a moral and educational significance: they created conditions whereby people could work and even enter into conflict in a climate of mutual respect, safeguarding the customary forms of the civilized world. Thus, they did not lose faith in themselves and could feel that human values had remained intact, that this whole catastrophe was merely temporary and they would have only to wait for the dawn of liberation.

I imposed order and maintained certain rules of conduct for the Central Commission of Tenement Committees with a tenacity bordering on the pedantic. The meetings were regularly held every Tuesday at 5:00 P.M. and never started later than 5:15. As the members of different Jewish institutions can attest, such punctiliousness is a fairly rare manifestation of social discipline. Those members kept from attending the meeting had to apprise the commission of the fact and justify their absence. Usually, everyone expected to participate was present. These may seem trifling concerns, but in the period of the ghetto, when the whole world seemed to have gone mad and to be hurtling toward an abyss, established rules gave us an awareness of the stability of moral values and the feeling that social duty toward our people was a real obligation that had to guide all our conduct.

This idea was understood and appreciated in every social circle in the ghetto. One day I ran into Giterman on Leszno Street, around five in the afternoon; and he greeted me with: "Ah! It must be Tuesday." These "Tuesdays" were maintained for all of 1941 and the first half of 1942. The last meeting took place on July 17, 1942. Naturally, the start of the *Große Aktion* put an end to our organization.

Certain elements in the welfare institutions, notably those that sought to consolidate power in their own hands and wield it without any outside supervision, were ironical about my activities in this sphere, accusing me of playing at English-style parliamentarianism. I would answer them that, yes, from a certain point of view, it was indeed a game; but one I preferred to the game of authoritarian totalitarianism.

Though we directed the activities of the Tenement Committees, we had no funds at our disposal. I remember that, on hearing of extreme distress among some of our active colleagues, I had to speak to the official administrative apparatus of Mutual Aid. After lengthy negotiations, shortly before July 15, 1942, fairly insubstantial packages of food supplies were made available to us—an allotment that came sporadically at that.

The authority of the Central Commission of Tenement Committees was purely moral, and whenever the official welfare organization wished to undertake some campaign requiring broad public participation, it did not do so without the approval of our commission, knowing that it would otherwise be bound to fail. That is true, for instance, of the above-mentioned plan to confiscate 30,000 food cards, and of the project for Winter Relief, 1941–42: the *Judenrat* required the campaign to be launched in its name, and generally sabotaged it from the outset. Finally, this latter project was submitted to the Central Commission, which posed precise stipulations to have the Tenement Committees participate in this action.

Likewise, I remember the following case: We were requested one day to go immediately to the *KOM* where an urgent decision had to be made. At the moment I was in our headquarters, in the company of A. Landau and the lawyer Szulman. We left for the offices of *KOM*, where the organization's full committee had assembled, together with the representatives of all the political parties and a delegate from the *Judenrat*. The reason for the emergency meeting was this: an edict had been issued, threatening to apply the death penalty to any Jewish person who crossed the borders of the ghetto. Some days later, nineteen people (most of them teenagers) were arrested for this criminal offense and transferred to the ghetto prison, where they awaited imminent execution. Technical preparations were under way: the Germans, apparently, wanted to have the executions carried out by the Polish police; the latter refused, and finally the Germans were taking it upon themselves to shoot the detainees in the presence of the Polish police. What was certain is that this catastrophe could occur any second. Given this situation, the Gestapo struck a bargain with the *Judenrat*: if fifteen hundred fur-lined jackets were provided for the German army, the "fate of the nineteen convicts could be reconsidered." We were faced with a most painful case of conscience: were we to persevere in our line of conduct that ruled out any aid to the Germans and condemn nineteen living beings, or save them by accepting a compromise? I can still remember the basic tenor of the ensuing debate. As in any other setting, it took place in a gathering that included people without will or resolution, who were trying simply to fulfill their responsibility. They maintained that the Germans would not dare to shoot adolescents for so small a misdemeanor (such illusions persisted among some people even as late as 1942), but most had a very clear opinion, which they took no pains to conceal. It was a clash of two diametrically opposed opinions, and oddly enough they were expressed by members of the same party (the General Zionists). Kirszenbaum categorically stated that any abetting of the Germans had to be ruled out, even if it meant losing nineteen men—whom we had to regard as soldiers who had fallen at the front, like countless other Allied soldiers who were meeting their deaths on the world's battlefields. E. Bloch took an opposite stance. Invoking humanitarian principles, the Bible, the value Judaism attributes to human life, he considered that the demands of the Germans had to be met. As for the *Judenrat*, it wanted not only to procure the jackets for the Germans, but to give the collection for the purchase of those jackets the semblance of a large popular action, by enlisting the participation of the Tenement Committees, which explained our inclusion in the meeting. I refused any cooperation on our part, stressing how demoralizing such a campaign would be. But, on the other hand, I considered the promise of the Germans to pardon nineteen prisoners in exchange for fifteen hundred fur-lined jackets to be a mere whim on their part, to be turned to advantage: they could just as well demand five thousand, and had in fact already taken all our fur clothes without giving us anything in exchange. If their proposal was accepted, the funds would have either to be taken from the coffers of the *Judenrat*, or gathered by taking up a collection among a very limited number of people.

The meeting ended there, but I learned later that the convicts had been released—the *Judenrat* had thus accepted the terms of the bargain. But to characterize the mentality of the Warsaw *Judenrat*, let me further point out the following fact: Several days later, I received a printed invitation from the *Judenrat* to attend a "celebration on the occasion of the happy outcome of an action." I didn't attend, but other people who did go to the festivities told me that it was indeed a celebration for the release of the nineteen death-row prisoners at the cost of supplying fur-lined jackets for the German army. Guests were served a dinner washed down with wines, and the speeches delivered sang the praises of our wise guardians and saviors in the *Judenrat*. Proof of what aberrations lack of tact and understanding can breed!

The Central Commission of Tenement Committees had become the parliament of the Public Sector. Its moral influence exceeded the limits of its formal competence and extended, to some degree, to all the relief agencies. The most active community workers in the districts were represented in it. Our parliamentarians of the Central Commission were obliged to carry on their work in the districts; in turn, the community workers of the districts took active part in the efforts of the Tenement Committees. In this way, by the very structure of the Public Sector, the members of the highest authority—the Central Commission—were not isolated from the masses and extended their activity both to the districts and to the committees of their tenements.

The Tenement Committees were so deeply rooted in the life of the ghetto that its existence is inconceivable without them. An entire folklore sprang up around these committees, a series of anecdotes underscored their role. They have faded from my memory, but I do recall one joke: when a woman was trying to justify her prolonged absence, she did not use the traditional excuse of stopping at the dressmaker's, but the pretext of consulting the secretary of the Tenement Committee.

If it were possible to establish statistics for what the Tenement Committees managed to accomplish, the results would be quite impressive. Unfortunately, all these data were swallowed up in the total destruction; there is less chance of retrieving them than there is of reconstructing any area of prehistoric culture through excavations. The destruction of the ghetto was carried out so relentlessly that excavations would be quite useless.

Just as it is not possible to reproduce any final reckoning of the activity of the Tenement Committees, it is impossible to relate the multiple spheres of their activity and the individual nature of certain committees, which differed appreciably from one another.

So I shall limit myself to describing, for the sake of illustration, the activity of the Tenement Committee in my building at 32 Elektoralna Street, which will give an idea of the committees of well-off apartment houses. In addition to the aid given to tenants at this address, the committee provided funds to support the Refugee Center at 12 Elektoralna Street, which was directed by two ladies who were members of the committee. A collective kitchen was created and was functional for a certain length of time, offering highly nutritious meals for free to indigent tenants, and to all the others at cost. The residents regularly paid monthly dues, with collections taken up in urgent cases. For his part, the committee president, a very well-off man, gave extensive help to the needy. The committee had a meeting space, made up of three rooms, which lent it the character of a club. Every evening, the tenants gathered there, a buffet was available to them, and they played cards at several tables. A certain percentage of the money wagered went to the committee, as did the revenue from the buffet. The committee sometimes organized evenings with invited guests, with considerable profits.

For all the effectiveness of these measures, the prevailing atmosphere in this committee was rather lukewarm. True enthusiasm, all the more touching because it roused people who themselves were weary and wretched, could be found in certain tenements of the poor. In these buildings, instead of donating part of their surplus, the inhabitants shared their very last resources with others. In certain cases, the solidarity manifested by the tenants of the poorest tenements was very moving. Unfortunately, the hundreds of cases that would demonstrate this attitude elude me now, relegating my remarks to generalities rather than concrete and convicing images.

All the same, I hope to have given an accurate picture of the genuine nature of this extraordinary popular movement created by the Public Sector in the Warsaw ghetto, as well as of the frame of mind in which the vast majority of its community workers functioned. I would not like my readers, however, to have the impression that I am giving more than their due to the people of that Sector, or going out of my way to set off their untarnished brightness against the black background that surrounded them. No, the Public Sector was composed of human beings who lived, for the most part, in very wretched conditions and who were not without human shortcomings. If corruption did not exist in the Sector, at times perceptible personal ambitions certainly came into play. The immediate concerns of their tenement building or their district would mask for them the breadth of the problem we had to resolve, and in tackling these problems it was necessary to wage a vigorous struggle against excessive localism. But these details have little significance when seen against the larger picture, reflecting the understanding, altruistic, and humanitarian spirit that guided the Public Sector and that had given birth to institutions that were unique in kind, created in the equally unique conditions of the Warsaw ghetto.

XI. A GHETTO "TOURIST GUIDE"

Despite a life without hope or prospects, people in the Warsaw ghetto never fully lost their sense of humor—black humor, at least—reflecting the day-to-day tragedy of this city cut off from the outer world.

One manifestation of this humor was the circulation, in handwritten editions, of the *Tourist Guide to the Ghetto*, the work of an unknown author. Outwardly, this tourist guide read like a brochure inviting visitors to the monuments and attractions of any city in the world. The top of the page bore an inscription in French:

"Visitez le ghetto, ses portes and ses ponts, goûtez son délicieux 'czoulent', admirez ses 'armoires musicales', ses rues animées . . . ." [Visit the ghetto, its gates and its bridges, sample its delicious *tsolent*, marvel at its "musical cupboards," its lively streets . . . .]

Every section of this text requires explanations, since the content in no way corresponds to what foreign tourists are normally led to visit.

The gates of the ghetto were not relics of antiquity and bore no stamp of hallowed ages, but were, on the contrary, the work of the most advanced totalitarian technology: each was guarded outside by German sentinels and inside by the Jewish police, effectively sealing a half-million condemned people into a virtual death-site. Only rarely did these gates open: to allow some German or Pole to enter on official business and to let out gangs of Jewish workers or the important members of the *Judenrat*, who possessed individual passes. Occasionally, by expending great effort, isolated persons would manage to obtain a pass granting a single trip out into the Aryan city of Warsaw. These passes were highly coveted and were obtained either through the protection of the *Judenrat*, or by bribery. Personally, I hadn't the least desire to venture, even for a few hours, into Aryan Warsaw. During my whole stay in the ghetto, I crossed over only once to visit the German Jews who had been sent to Warsaw early in the spring of 1942. They were being housed in a school building outside the ghetto. The group of community workers to which I belonged went there accompanied by a guard. The several hours I spent among these Jews from Hanover, Göttingen, and the Rhineland cities, are still vivid in my memory. I recall a young woman painter, a native of Hanover. Unlike the others, she had very little baggage with her, but was happy to have been able to bring along her copy of *Faust*. In one of the rooms, Doctor Bloch, also from Hanover, had spread out before him a whole assortment of medical instruments and lavished his professional care on his compatriots. Although each room contained at least forty people, the order that reigned there was exemplary: each family occupied a designated place, the suitcases were neatly arranged, and the overcoats hung on the wall. I had occasion to speak one-by-one with ten people. For me, having come straight out of the ghetto, this was contact with the outer world. What struck me was the air of healthiness and optimism of the entire group, as well as an absence of any sign of fear for their fate. The young people were dancing to music from a phonograph. Everyone was asking the same questions: was there work to be had in the ghetto (where they expected to be transferred soon)? Was the housing clean? Was there any fear of heavy bombings?

In the ghetto, on the other hand, the arrival of this group roused some apprehension among certain circles, who feared that the Germans might make the newcomers their tools and grant them privileged conditions.

Unfortunately, neither these fears nor the concerns of the German Jews had any basis. In the course of the second night of their stay in Warsaw, 140 of the youngest among them, by a roll call, were deported to Treblinka (which at this time was believed to be a labor camp); and soon after, the others from the Land of the Masters disappeared in turn.

The bridges of the ghetto had an even more remarkable and ultramodern character, for they were not built for crossing water, but passed over streets that did not belong to the ghetto and were off-limits to Jews. The main bridge was erected above Chlodna Street; it linked the two parts of Zelazna Street that intersected it and served as the only passage between the "big" and "little" ghettos.

On this bridge crowds of people would circulate in both directions with the greatest difficulty, in an indescribable crush. One day I chanced to observe this movement from the window of the house alongside it. The impression was at once eerie and grotesque, comparable to some movie newsreel showing dense masses of Chinese fleeing from an overflowing river.

Still, this bridge did not exist from the outset. Earlier, the two perpendicular streets—the Aryan Chlodna Street and the Jewish Zelazna Street—were separated by heavy iron gates, guarded by the Germans and opening alternately for the passage of Aryans and Jews. In its Aryan part, Chlodna

Street had little commotion on it, the gates stayed open most of the time and the traffic flowed without congestion. But on Zelazna Street, which served as the only link between two parts of the ghetto, and where the Jews were in constant circulation, the gates opened only rarely, and very briefly. Once they opened them, the German policemen kept the crowd moving to the beat of their riding crops, which created an atmosphere of panic. On approaching this intersection, the Jews could not help but feel feverish agitation. The crowd would pack in, and everyone would try to squeeze inside in order not to be exposed to the blows of the Germans. For this reason, movement slowed, and the riding crops came down all the more furiously on the hapless outsiders. What is more, it was routine for these defenseless people to be humiliated. The policemen would pick some poor wretch from the crowd at random, and force him to do calisthenics while beating him mercilessly, or in winter make him kneel in the puddles of melting snow.

The construction of the bridge improved this situation. Crossing it, we could get a glimpse of the Aryan street, spacious and clean, where traffic was normal, where cars wheeled by and trolley cars passed . . . while we were separated by an abyss from these simple manifestations of daily urban life . . . .

Another nerve center of the ghetto was Karmelicka Street, which, before the war, had been a very busy commercial thoroughfare in the Jewish quarter. The streets parallel to it on both sides were Aryan, and it was the only passageway into the most populous part of the ghetto. Unfortunately, it also offered a very convenient path toward the historic Pawiak prison, which had been renowned in the period of revolutionary struggle and stood at the ghetto's border. To get there, the German trucks took this route. The street was very narrow, and the Germans, armed with wooden or iron sticks whose length reached both sidewalks, would amuse themselves, from atop their trucks, by hitting passersby over the head. Many received skull fractures. On hearing the trucks approach, people would flee on all sides and hide under the carriage entrances, but the narrowness of the street forced them to huddle together, creating an excellent target for the Germans.

To bypass this street, an inner passage was devised by connecting adjacent courtyards, so that one could pass from Nowolipki Street into Leszno Street. Street vendors set up their stalls in this passageway. The bottleneck and the crush that resulted were impossible to describe.

In getting around the ghetto, it was inevitable to encounter German sentinels at certain boundary points. There was one such area at the intersection of Leszno and Zelazna Streets, where an abominable, brute-faced giant was posted; the Jews had nicknamed him "Frankenstein." For sport, this beast would thrash passersby with the butt of his rifle and even open fire on them. At such close range a human target was easy to hit; each little spree ended with a victim fallen on the ground.

Nonetheless, all these dangers were only episodic. The essential feeling you got from the ghetto streets was the despair of an involuntarily sealed-off world.

Moving on to the next sections of our "Tourist Guide," I shall mention that the *tsolent* was a very rich item of Jewish ritual food, eaten on Saturdays. In the ghetto, given the scarcity of fat in the diet, this dish was considered a national delicacy.

The "musical cupboards" had a highly specific meaning. The expression "the cupboard is playing" meant that someone had bribed the police, or greased their palms. The phrase became so common that in speaking of some scheme that had worked (a smuggling job, for instance) it was simply said that "the cupboard's played." As for the police, they also promised to fulfill their end of the bargain by saying: "if the cupboard plays." The origin of this expression may be explained as follows: in the past, shady deals had been worked out with officials in the cabarets, which had mechanical music boxes in the shape of cupboards. When a coin was put into the slot, the music box would start playing a song. The connection is very clear: you pay, and we'll do what's necessary. In the prewar years I had never heard this expression. The reason it was revived and became so widespread in the ghetto remains one of the mysteries of social psychology.

At its conclusion the "Tourist Guide" mentions the ghetto's bustling streets: yes, these streets were much-traveled, but they were also like nothing else found in any other city in the world.

For the streets of any of any other city in the world lead somewhere. They form part of the vast world to which they connect their cities. They open the way to freedom. By walking along them, one can come out at the broad avenues at the center of town or, on the contrary, emerge into the fields, the forests, onto the banks of rivers . . . . The streets of the ghetto led nowhere. They came up against an insurmountable wall, or a German sentinel. All the streets of the ghetto were dead ends, and the people thronging them amid the tumult and the stench found themselves facing that impasse: they had nowhere to go, could find no exit . . . .

Sometimes, certain ghetto streets—the ones that were off-limits—completely disappeared; and some connecting artery which, just the evening before had been in its rightful place, suddenly ceased to exist. It was necessary then to look for new routes over the maze of walls and the rifles of the German sentinels: in the process, some destination previously seven or eight minutes away now took at least a half hour to walk.

For the first year of its existence the ghetto still had a functioning trolley line, staffed by Poles, which gave the ghetto the illusion of resembling a normal city. But the ride in a trolley car often turned into a trap. In the Aryan part of the city, the conductors and the public had joined together to sabotage the German officials: Either the passengers would simply not pay for their tickets, or the same ticket would be used by several people—stepping off the tram, the passenger would give his ticket to the conductor, who then passed it on to the next person boarding. This system did not exist in the ghetto, where the Polish conductors showed no solidarity with the Jews. Tickets were paid for with small coins, a great many of them forged and quite hard to tell from real ones. When a Jew happened to give the conductor a fake coin, the latter would use this for blackmail: he would demand a certain sum of money, threatening otherwise to report the passenger to the Germans. This cannot be said of all the conductors, but such cases were not rare; several of my friends were victims of this practice.

Later, the trolley line was eliminated because it passed through border streets one side of which, belonging still to the Aryan part of the city, now officially lay beyond the ghetto. Walls were erected where the rails had been. The Germans assumed that the border-zone apartment houses, whose courtyards flanked those of the Aryans, would make it easy for ghetto inhabitants to communicate clandestinely with the outer world—which in fact was the case. The construction of the walls now isolated the ghetto completely.

After the trolley line was removed, the only means of mass transportation that survived in the ghetto were a few horse-drawn omnibuses (of the firm Kohn & Heller) and a certain number of bicycles with trailers. This was decidedly not enough, and the vast majority of the population went about on foot.

On the streets, the passersby tried not to get too close to one another, to keep from picking up lice, the carriers of typhus. This, though, was wasted effort, and, on coming home, one often found one's clothes infested with these disgusting, dangerous vermin, the inevitable accompaniment of wars and times of distress. At first we were alarmed and anxiously counted the days of the incubation period for typhus; but as time went on, whenever we went out into the street, we came to accept this everyday risk and paid it no further heed.

Certain main thoroughfares in the ghetto were always congested; this was a city with a lack of space not only in housing, but in the streets as well. Also, the mentality and the appearance of the crowd differed from those of other cities in the world, where people may step out to take walks, to get a bit of air, or to take care of various business. In the ghetto it was impossible to breathe fresh air—this was the quarter of Warsaw completely bereft of vegetation, with neither gardens nor squares. You could count the number of trees, all of them sickly, that did grow there. The stench of the ghetto's streets made it difficult to breathe. Most of the residents had no business that induced them to leave their houses, and it was only the despair and living conditions in those overcrowded apartments that forced them out into the street. Amid the crowd, however, they found a great feeling of security. Yet the most powerful motive that forced them out-of-doors was hunger. The streets were overrun with vendors of different foods or people driven to sell off their own goods or property. And despite this, the sense of humor always remained lively: I remember a poor old man who was selling a few oranges on Solna Street, hawking his merchandise with the cry: "Jews, buy oranges! It's incredible—there are even oranges in the ghetto!"

A characteristic group among the merchants were the second-hand dealers who sold books in every possible language, displayed on their handcarts.

But the two sovereign powers ruling the streets of the ghetto were typhus and hunger—fierce, piercing, degrading hunger. Young boys, not yet robbed of their vitality, would resort to direct action, getting their nourishment by sheer force. Every day one could see boys stealing up like wolves to passersby carrying any sort of food (but especially bread), deftly snatching it away from them, and starting in at once to devour their booty, even as they fled. Usually these passersby would simply mourn their loss and continue on. But sometimes what the robbery victim had lost was the last morsel of bread meant for a hungry family; visibly desperate, he would try to catch up with his assailant and recover the precious nourishment. One day on Leszno Street I observed the following scene: A poor man, with a drawn face, had caught the thief, whose escape a Jewish policeman was blocking. The boy fell and the policeman began battering him. The man was trying to grab the piece of bread from the boy, who, oblivious to the blows, would not let go and continued to devour it.

With the adults and the elderly, whose sufferings had reduced their strength, hunger manifested itself passively: they
begged alms . . . .

Nowhere was the number of beggars higher than in the
ghetto. These hordes of ragged beggars, men, women, old
people, and children, with desperate faces and swollen limbs,
made the ghetto streets look like a cross between an Oriental
bazaar and a lunatic asylum. Some of them begged alone, others in groups or in families; some merely held out their hands,
others wept, sang, and danced; empty cans of preserves,
banged together, served as their instruments. Many had obviously been driven mad by hunger. An entire folklore of
hunger, now forgotten, sprang up in the ghetto. I remember a
random couplet sung by various beggars near our building:

> *Unser prezesowe mach a ondoulazie*
> *Und ich hob gor nicht off kilatzie,*
> *Oj, hinger, hinger, hinger!*

Meaning: The wife of our president (of the *Judenrat*) gets a
permanent, / While I can't get a meal, / Oh! hunger, hunger,
hunger!

Let me point out in this regard that the wife of President
Czerniakow, whom the beggars no doubt did not know, was
in reality a modest, decent woman who devoted most of her
time to helping children.

A special category of beggars were those—and their ranks
never ceased to grow—who said nothing, but simply exhib-
ited their swollen limbs. It was only in the depths of the
ghetto that I understood the Russian expression "to blow up
with hunger." Malnutrition makes one thin and pale, but
true hunger produces the opposite effect; the victim starts to

swell up, above all in the legs, which take on the appearance of bulging blisters and are covered with shiny, red skin, as though coated with fat.

As if it were yesterday, I can see before me the image of one of these wretches. He was a schoolteacher from the provinces; he had the same family name as one of the relief workers in our district, and although the latter did not know him, he would sometimes come to visit him as though he were a relative. Later, I saw this man begging on Leszno Street. Two weeks later he was still in the same spot, his trousers rolled up very high, appealing for charity by the sight of his puffed-up legs. Not long after, he was seated, still in the same place, having lost the ability to stand up. Then, he disappeared—like so many others. Alas! generations of beggars vanished, one after the other, at an accelerated pace; often, they would collapse in the street, where their corpses would remain for several days, covered by old newspapers; for they were too numerous and people had no time to bury them fast enough in anonymous tombs.

Other beggars took the place of those who vanished, their numbers continually rose, but life went on—this life that was one long agony in the City of Death, where the fatal days of July 1942 were approaching.

XII. FORECAST: APOCALYPSE

In mid-June of 1942 a rumor was suddenly, insistently spreading through the ghetto, filling everyone's hearts with premonitions of horrors to come. This rumor was simple and unequivocal: in the "Aryan" city of Warsaw there were posters hung up that read: "40 Days of Jewish Life." The sources for this story were Poles who came to the ghetto on service matters and the Jews who had passes to go into Warsaw. I asked a friend about it who often went into the Aryan city. He had seen no such posters. Despite everything, the rumor continued to spread. We were in a period when, even with hermetically sealed borders, some information about mass exterminations of the Jews in eastern Poland had made its way into the ghetto. Although the Jews refused to believe this news, simply dismissing the reports, the atmosphere of general anxiety allowed the posting of such a public notice to be interpreted as a proclamation of the planned extermination of the Warsaw ghetto.

All this was totally absurd: the Germans never announced their plans; on the contrary, they kept them secret so that unpredictability could cripple any attempts at resistance. However, in the helpless confusion of the time, the posters aroused Jews' attention.

At the same time, various strange events occurred in the ghetto. German movie crews appeared and filmed displays in grocery store windows, after first forcing the owners to decorate them with great care and stock them with rare and expensive commodities. Next, they set about filming the well-furnished apartments, above all in Chlodna Street, where certain members of the *Judenrat* lived, and well-off people in general. They would select the best-furnished rooms, where they could find at least one pretty and well-dressed young woman. This was carried out without great brutality. I recall one case in which an assigned extra had refused to play her part. She was replaced by another, more conciliatory lady.

Nevertheless, even this movie campaign did not go off without a few barbaric episodes: Thus, a number of Orthodox-looking men were forcibly piled into the ritual bath (*mikva*) with several young women. They were all forced to strip completely, and filmed as though they were bathing together.

Here is another episode of this filmmaking saga: the Germans ordered the owner of the Restaurant Schulz (at the corner of Karmelicka and Nowolipki Streets) to set an abundant spread of food and drink at every table. Then they brought in Jews picked at random off the street. They were ordered to take their places at these tables and eat. This feast was then filmed. The restaurateur was told to send the bill to the *Judenrat*.

It so happened I was visiting the premises of Mutual Aid, at 29a Nowolipki Street, precisely when some Jews who had taken part in this feast came in. They told us with astonishment what had happened. With the sense of humor I've said remained intact in the ghetto, we joked that this was the first time the *Judenrat* was forced actually to feed the hungry.

Some days later the filming in the ghetto ended, but it did not stop worrying us. We were lost in conjecture about its meaning. Without a doubt, the Germans wanted to give life in the ghetto a false, tendentious appearance, presenting it as a place of debauchery and social injustice. But why?

Some people drew a connection between these facts and the infamous posters about the "40 Days of Jewish Life": Surely the film was meant to offer moral justification for extermination of the Jewish Sodom.

But then people came up with another, more optimistic, explanation: The Germans were preparing a film about life in the ghetto, and the posters were merely the announcement for this film. Thus, in the minds of many people, the terrible announcement of extermination was transformed into movie publicity. Finally, in the fitful, harrowing life of the ghetto, the posters and filming alike were forgotten.

But on July 22, the day the *Große Aktion* began, there were many who remembered that the rumor of "40 Days of Jewish Life" had started up exactly that many days before the fatal day.

Later, when I found myself outside the borders of the ghetto, pretending to be an Aryan, I made further investigations, but no one had ever seen the famous posters, and it can be stated with certainty that they never existed.

Were the frayed nerves of the ghetto residents endowed with a sixth sense that prompted this collective presentiment?

Whatever its cause, the mystery surrounding the origin of this rumor and its prophetic exactness will never be fully explained.

XIII. THE *GROßE AKTION* BEGINS (JULY 1942)

As time went on, life in the ghetto grew more and more feverish, shaken by the sudden bolts of despair and vain hopes. Our terrible reality fed on ever more terrifying rumors. At first, stories started circulating about mobile gas chambers in which Jews were being exterminated in the western regions of Poland. Basically, though, no one believed these rumors. Then, in the spring of 1942, news filtered in that masses of Jews in eastern Poland were being deported to an unknown destination, especially those in the province of Lublin, and not just the native Jews but also those who had already been deported from Czechoslovakia and Germany. Then we learned, in more exact detail, that the entire Jewish population of the city of Lublin—more than forty thousand people—had vanished. The official version of the transfer of Jews to "the East," into labor camps, seemed to be confirmed by widespread reports in Warsaw concerning letters certain ghetto residents had supposedly received from relatives and friends transferred .to Bialystok, Minsk, and other cities, where they were said to be working under decent conditions, etc.

I personally looked into a certain number of these rumors, asking the person I was speaking with for the source of his information. I would then go to that source and pursue my investigations, which would invariably reach a dead end: the person or address cited did not exist. It is highly possible that such rumors were consciously started by German agents and caught in passing by ghetto residents, who went about looking for even the faintest glimmer of hope. In reality, though, all news of the letters received by deported relatives was pure invention. In this period, during a meeting of relief workers that took place on the premises of the people's kitchen on Orla Street, I attempted to ask the question in all its appalling obviousness: Was it possible that none of the forty thousand Jewish inhabitants of Lublin had sent news of themselves to their relatives in Warsaw? In the regions occupied by the Germans (including the ghetto) the mail was functioning fairly normally. It was still possible to communicate by means of railwaymen or other civil servants. However, not a single piece of news had come from Lublin, and we had to reckon with the evidence: the entire Jewish population of this city had disappeared without a trace.

But if, on the one hand, it was impossible not to be aware of this horrifying reality, at once absurd and ineluctable, on the other hand, there remained a basic subconscious optimism, inherent in every human soul, that refused to believe in the hell that had been created on earth. The entire Jewish population of Warsaw was imbued with this hope, in various forms and degrees. And even those among us who admitted that the massacre of the Jews of Lublin was an incontestable fact, and who had to concede that we too were in the same predicament and had no reason to expect different treatment by the Germans—dismissed, despite everything, the idea of a possible extermination of the Warsaw ghetto, unwilling to acknowledge that our situation was desperate.

In the suffocating atmosphere that still never ceased to worsen as the nightmare loomed closer, the ghetto continued its convulsive day-to-day existence: People clung to life and intensified their efforts to avoid dying of hunger. The social institutions rallied their available forces, and the whole tottering edifice held together, thanks only to an extreme nervous tension and the longing to survive at any cost until the moment of liberation—in which we had unshakable faith. I stress once more this essential element in the mentality of the ghetto; for without it, existence would have been impossible and inconceivable.

Against all evidence, people refused to believe in the inhuman schemes that were being perpetrated in the world. I recall a conversation I had at a moment when the *Große Aktion* was at its height. There were more than a thousand of us crammed into the small carpentry shop of the Landau brothers on Gesia Street. By this time we already had precise information about the fate of the deportees. The women and children still alive remained hidden for days on end behind fake walls, which had been erected out of wooden crates. After one such day on which a terrible roundup had taken place, some of us met in the evening at the plant's office. One of the men speaking, a history professor whose name escapes me, but whose waxen face and blazing, evasive eyes live etched in my memory, tried to persuade us that we were all under the influence of a pessimistic psychosis that was distorting our sense of reality. He countered all our objections concerning the confirmed, incontestable facts with countless examples from different historical periods in which people succumbed to a collective psychosis of anxiety before a nonexistent danger . . . . He spoke garrulously, nervously, as though he wished above all to persuade himself. Alas! reality defeated him: soon after this conversation our preacher was himself taken in a roundup.

At this stage, we already knew with certainty what deportation meant. We had managed to ascertain it in the following way: the numbers of the dispatched cars were posted at the site from which convoys departed (the *Umschlagplatz*), and we could determine from these that the same cars came back empty twelve to fourteen hours later; there was the proof that they had not made a long journey toward the East. We learned of the existence of Treblinka from a Polish railwayman, who had a female in-law who had been deported there. The man had spent several days in this region, so by his own observations as well as the stories of farmers from those parts, he verified that they were transporting thousands of people every day into the camp, people who were not being supplied with food—on the contrary, they were having whole transports sent out of the camp with clothing and personal effects. There could be no further doubt about the fate of the deportees. Finally, one day, a young man showed up at the carpentry shop who had managed to escape from Treblinka. He had stayed alive, working for some days in a commando unit assigned to bury the corpses. One evening a large convoy of Jews from the city of Radom arrived unexpectedly at Treblinka, which created a certain confusion in the camp. He used the occasion to escape and return to the ghetto.

At the start of the *Aktion* there were many who calmly prepared themselves for departure: They gathered their traveling clothes, packed easily transportable bags, debated over what currency to take with them for their expenses in the "work" sites, etc.

Likewise I can recall a conversation, at the start of the *Aktion*, with the leader of the leftist faction of the *Poalei-Zion* Party, Szachne Sagan, and Dr. Ringelblum. I was of the opinion that everyone should be informed of the fate that awaited us and, since we had no other means of defense, should storm the gates of the ghetto in a crowd of several hundreds of thousands, make our way past the sentinels and then scatter into the Aryan city. Obviously, I was aware that the vast majority would be massacred, but it might just be possible for a certain number to make it into hiding. I thought we had nothing to lose, since the extermination awaiting us would necessarily be total.

My interlocutors replied that there was hope of saving a part of the population, that it had not been proven that the Germans intended to carry out a total extermination, that they took into consideration certain exemption papers. As an example, they cited the city of Rovno, where some twenty thousand Jews were brutally massacred, yet where six to seven thousand artisans together with their families lived and worked in tranquility, etc.

The official version, which came to us through the Jewish police collaborating with the German deportation staff, was that only a part, the "surplus" population, was destined for deportation. Initially, it was stated that 300,000 Jews would remain in the ghetto; for this reason, the *Judenrat* was apparently involved in negotiations with the Germans to establish the number of the ghetto's Jews: The *Judenrat* was trying to reduce the count, whereas the Germans considered the number to be higher. As the *Aktion* continued without letup, rumors about the number of those who would remain gradually changed: people spoke of 250,000; 200,000; etc., until there was no further doubt that these rumors were unfounded and that the *Aktion* was limitless.

Nonetheless, the masses still did not believe in total extermination and did not lose hope that the *Aktion* would come to an end.

There is one scene I remember. It was seven or eight days after the start of the *Aktion*. We still had access to the premises of the sixth district of Mutual Aid, at 29 Nowolipki Street, and we often gathered there. This was the very day we received the tragic message from Wielikowski, to the effect that the *Aktion* was being stepped up and the daily contingent raised from ten to twelve thousand persons. We were walking down into the courtyard, still under the impact of this news; it was 5:00 P.M. on a lovely summer day. In the courtyard were massed a few hundred people who had deserted the streets, which seemed to them more dangerous, or who were nursing the illusion of being out of harm's way on Mutual Aid terrain. These people looked exhausted, they were starving, had not slept or been able to wash . . . . They were all sitting down or half stretched out, leaning against the walls or against their baggage. And yet at this moment, before my eyes, the crowd was literally transformed. Someone entered the courtyard shouting: "The *Aktion* is over, the Germans said so, they were passing in a car and announced it to us." These words went through the crowd like an electric current. Everyone got up, people rushed toward each other, repeating the words, first hesitantly, then with conviction: "The *Aktion* is ended, it's over."

Our small group tried to bring them back to their senses, but without any success; everyone was shouting: "It's over, it's over, the Germans said so."

People clustered together, some hugging, others laughing, some crying . . . .

The nervous tension soared, was transformed into ecstasy, took the form of a collective psychosis. It was a harrowing scene, indescribable, unforgettable . . . . It had not lasted long, at most fifteen to twenty minutes! Soon we heard whistles blowing—the Jewish police were not far away—a roundup was beginning.

The *Aktion* was continuing, had expanded, and from this day on was to be even more relentless.

Apartment houses, blocks of them, whole streets were emptied, and when the prey started dwindling, the raids and deportations extended to the protected factories and work-shops.

According to German sources, 316,822 people were de-ported from the Warsaw ghetto and exterminated between the start of 1942 and the end of January 1943. In reality, the number of victims must have been higher. Many perished on site, shot while trying to save themselves. In some cases whole families were massacred, having been found in their apartments despite the order to go down into the courtyard. The sentinels often shot into the crowd, on mere suspicion that someone wanted to break out of line, or simply to get the lines into better formation. After the roundups, numer-ous corpses would sometimes be left behind in our carpentry workshop.

Humanity has known dramas in which the victims were no fewer than in the Warsaw ghetto—the Battle of Verdun, for instance, and natural disasters—and has nothing to be proud of in the massacres and atrocities perpetrated in dif-ferent eras and various countries; but only in the twentieth century can it record the premeditated, thoroughly planned annihilation of countless masses of innocent people, through use of all the means of modern technology and all possibilities available to a state.

The twentieth century witnessed a new sort of crime, committed not by criminals or mobs of gangsters, but by the state: a state had perpetrated the most horrible of crimes—the annihilation of whole peoples—genocide. The first example of such a crime was the massacre of the Armenians by the Turks in 1915, in the course of the First World War.

During the terrible days of July and August 1942, we often spoke of the fate of the Armenians; most of us knew Werfel's book, *The Forty Days of Musa-Dagh,* and we often recalled an episode described in it—the arrival of French warships bringing aid to the Armenians. "But," we said, "we unfortunately cannot count on any aid, we are doomed, and no one's going to try to rescue us." This was in the period when Hitler occupied Europe from the Pyrenees to the Volga; thousands of kilometers separated us from the free world, delivering us up defenseless to the Nazi monster.

Free humanity had not fulfilled its duty to the Armenian martyrs; it had forgotten about this unprecedented crime and, with this fact, had fatefully committed a sin against itself.

And perhaps if, at the end of the First World War, a "Nuremberg Tribunal" had convened at Istanbul, the gas chambers and crematoria of Auschwitz and Treblinka would not have come into being.

In conditions of general impunity and indifference, the beast of apocalypse had reared its head and its insatiable entrails now clamored not for hundreds of thousands, but millions of victims. This time the victims were Jews; but if humanity does not put an end to these eruptions of bestiality, there is no telling whom this fate might befall on the next historical occasion.

"No one can deny the tragedy of the Jews, victims of the Germans"—a young Jewish doctor who had been in the French Resistance said to me one day—"but are we the only victims of the cruelties of modern war? Remember the bombing of German cities. I was there when Dresden was leveled by two air raids. And Hiroshima? Given these conditions, can we really single out our own Jewish martyrs?"

I tried to explain to him the essential difference of what had been perpetrated against the Jews. Obviously, we live in an epoch of unheard-of cruelty; firebombs dropped over German cities caused numberless casualties, but this was, after all, only a reprisal for what had been done to Warsaw, Rotterdam, Coventry, London, and other Allied cities. Hitler's Germany caused these actions, and therein may lie its chief crime (an idea formulated in the following way by Lecomte de Noüy in his book *La Dignité humaine*):

"Germany's crime is the greatest crime the world has ever known, because it is not on the scale of History: *it is on the scale of Evolution*" (p. 39). "It is thus in this that Germany's greatest crime consists, because as soon as one monster like this exists somewhere, it prompts the forming of other similar monsters by the necessity of self-protection and of safeguarding a material, cultural, and moral heritage: a vicious circle from which none can escape" (p. 44).

Hiroshima is a monstrous event; human thought can scarcely conceive that a single bomb would have been enough to wipe out several hundreds of thousands of peaceable Japanese. Undoubtedly, though, the supreme American command that gave the order, as well as the pilot who carried it out, considered this act an evil, albeit an inevitable one. Its goal was not to wipe out the peaceable Japanese population, but to end the war and to safeguard millions of human lives.

Human conscience, however, will not be appeased by this explanation. We face an insoluble moral dilemma: Why must precisely this Japanese child die to ransom with its blood other human lives? And what person has the right to assign this child its expiatory role?

In this unresolvable controversy, one thing is clear: The military operations of the Allies never had as an objective gratuitous atrocities. All free peoples considered the cruelties of the last war an evil they had not instigated, but which were inevitable.

And it is in this that those cruelties differ essentially from the German atrocities committed against the Jews: with the Nazis, the evil was the manifestation of a cult of bestiality that took on giant proportions; the evil among them was the actualization of their conception of the world and their diabolical program; it was the very essence of their nature. It was evil in pure form, an end in itself, evil for evil's sake.

It is inconceivable that this program directed against millions of defenseless human beings should have been accomplished with such merciless logic.

I can remember, in fact, an appalling scene: my wife and I were already hidden at the time in the carpentry shop of the Landau brothers. It was in the month of August, on a stifling day. The news had spread around us that on Gesia Street a large convoy of deportees was passing. We learned from a Jewish policeman that these were inhabitants of the little ghetto who were going to be eliminated. The little ghetto was made up of a few streets inhabited for the most part by well-to-do people and intellectuals. One of the buildings of the carpentry shop overlooked the street. Our small group walked up to the second floor and we started in secret to watch the street. It was a strange scene that unfolded before our eyes. The whole width of the street was filled with people. They were flanked by an escort composed of Jewish and German policemen. The escort was so broadly scattered that it sometimes passed unnoticed. Basically, there was, so to speak, almost nothing to look at: The prey was at the mercy of the hunter, with no means of escape. At the least suspicion he was about to flee, the suspect was shot point-blank. And even if someone managed to flee, he would inevitably have been found, a few days later, in the same ranks. The line of deportees was endless . . . . There were clearly thousands of victims. Though we could still see where this gruesome procession started, it was impossible to make out where it ended. The Germans were not rushed on this day—the contingent was more than complete—and they did not step up the march, as was usual. They were hot, too, and the street was very dusty . . . . People were moving ahead slowly, they did not walk in regular files but in groups or alone . . . . Sometimes one could see mothers leading little children by the hand, parents holding their babies in their arms. Some carried small packets, most had no baggage . . . . They had been taken by surprise. The women were wearing lightweight dresses, as though they had stepped out to take a stroll. We observed the crowd with dread. At times, we would recognize familiar faces, at times we seemed to glimpse people we knew . . . . But then it scarcely mattered whether we knew them or not . . . . This was the last road they would be taking on this earth, it was the last time we could see them . . . . It was quite hot, the people were tired and moving forward very slowly . . . . We could see neither the beginning not the end of the procession.

Perhaps some of them did not know what awaited them hours later, but they must have had grim forebodings and at the same time realize that what was happening to them was inevitable . . . . They had no way out . . . . And the most agonizing thing was the calm that emanated from this crowd of martyrs . . . .

Yet behind the walls that still protected us, we could not remain calm: We knew for certain that in an hour this entire crowd would be packed like cattle into freight cars, that after a 100-kilometer journey to Treblinka, they would be stripped and shoved into gas chambers, and that, a quarter of an hour later, on the other side, someone would be pulling out their corpses . . . . But the methodical workings of Hitler's machinery would not stop there: The hair that had graced these women's heads would serve in the manufacture of pillows, the gold teeth would be turned over to the *Reichsbank* to swell the Reich's coffers . . . . And the world would not have changed: that very day, in every city on earth, Warsaw included, people would go to the movies, or have a drink at a café, stop by their friends' for a hand of bridge . . . .

Surprise and at times blame have been voiced about the attitude of victims who went to their slaughter meekly and with resignation. But what were they to do? The world had forgotten them and tolerated their sacrifice. They had preferred to confront their ineluctable fate together, in calm and composure, supporting one another with this attitude of resignation. Not to submit was impossible. And this resignation on the part of the victims of the appalling, senseless schemes of a world gone mad was so magnificent a response, it makes any attempt to capture it in human words mere profanation.

XIV. THE *GROβE AKTION,* ITS PROGRESS, AND THE ROLE OF THE JEWISH POLICE

The *Große Aktion* in the Warsaw ghetto, i.e., the extermination of Europe's largest Jewish community, was prepared by the Germans in their typically systematic fashion; not a single detail of this vast plan was overlooked. Total extermination was first tried out on less populous communities, and only after minute preparations was the liquidating apparatus set in motion in Warsaw. It began with the creation, 120 kilometers from Warsaw, of a death camp—Treblinka. Gas chambers were installed there, provided with requisite quantities of *Cyklon B,* which modern German industry, the supplier of products for mass extermination, had perfected. In Warsaw itself, a deportation center (*Umschlagplatz*) was set up, linked to a junction of the rail-line and equipped with a sufficient quantity of rolling stock.

Rumors circulated among the Polish railwaymen involved in these labors that the freight cars were meant for the deportation of Jews. These rumors were brought to the attention of Czerniakow, the president of the *Judenrat,* by my friend Roman Lichtenbaum, a well-known lawyer, who later vanished mysteriously in the Aryan part of the city during the general insurrection in Warsaw in 1944. Czerniakow went to see the Gestapo, who categorically assured him the stories were unfounded. Obviously, one cannot place much trust in the Gestapo, yet one also cannot rule out the assumption that the local Gestapo had not been advised of the extermination plans for the Warsaw ghetto until the last moment.

Be that as it may, it was not the local Gestapo and the SS who were ordered to carry out the *Aktion*, but rather a team of murderers especially trained by Himmler and Globocnik. Some two weeks before the arrival of this team, a comfortable house was requisitioned at the ghetto border on Zelazna Street. It was set up with furnishings taken from Jewish apartments in the ghetto, and many domestics were taken on. They had no qualms about using Jewish manpower: a lady I knew was hired as a cook. Once all the furnishings had been moved in, the Extermination Commando arrived in Warsaw, and the signal for *Aktion* was given.

By order of the Germans, on July 22, 1942, the *Judenrat* posted the followed notice:

WARSAW JUDENRAT
NOTICE

Warsaw the 22nd of July, 1942

1. By order of the German authorities, all Jews residing in Warsaw, regardless of age and sex, will be deported to the East.

2. The following categories are exempt from the deportation order:

a) All Jews employed by the German authorities or by German employers and able to produce sufficient proof of this fact.

b) All Jews who are members or employees of the Judenrat, in accordance with their situation on the day of publication of the present order.

c) All Jews employed in firms belonging to Germans and able to produce sufficient proof of this fact.

d) All Jews not provided with such jobs, but able to work. They will be barracked in the Jewish quarter.

e) All Jews belonging to the Jewish civil police.

f) All Jews on the staffs of Jewish hospitals or Jewish disinfection teams.

g) All Jews related to persons who come under categories a) through f). Only wives and children are considered relatives.

h) All Jews who, on the day of deportation, are being cared for in Jewish hospitals, with the exception of those able to be moved. Inability to be moved must be certified by a physician designated by the Judenrat.

3. Every Jew to be included in deportation is authorized to take with him for the journey 15 kilos worth of personal effects. Anything exceeding 15 kilos will be confiscated. All objects of value, such as money, jewelry, gold, etc., may be brought along. It is necessary to take enough food for a three-day journey.

4. The deportation begins on July 22, 1942, at 11:00 A.M.

5. Sanctions:

a) Any Jew who does not belong to categories a) and c) and has no right to be included in them, who leaves the

Jewish quarter after deportation has commenced, will be shot.

b) Any Jew who undertakes acts that may hinder or prevent the execution of orders of deportation will be shot.

c) Any Jew lending support to those acts that may hinder or prevent the execution of orders of deportation will be shot.

d) Any Jew found in Warsaw after the end of the deportation of Jews and not to be included among the persons specified in categories a) through h) will be shot.

The morning of this sinister day is etched into my memory: once more I see the brick-red posters glued up beside one another, and the groups of panic-stricken people reading them.

Some days later, there appeared a new notice from the *Judenrat* promising three kilos of bread and one kilo of jam to those who would show up willingly at the *Umschlagplatz*. A modest price for a human life! But it was an accurate calculation: So many people were hungry and wretched, with no way out, a good number of volunteers swallowed the bait.

Coming back to this first notice, which was the essential act, or as it were the "constitution" of the deportation, we can observe that its most important point was to establish certain categories of people who apparently could not be deported. Was this from the very outset a conscious hoax on the part of the Germans, a psychological ruse meant to break the unity of the masses and any attempts at resistance, by giving every Jew the hope of being admitted into the privileged categories; or rather, did the Germans really first envisage retaining those who could work, and only later, as their butchery commenced, start to exterminate even those Jews who, in their opinion, could be useful to them? We shall not attempt to resolve this question. It still holds true here that the notion of self-preservation—torture by hope— played a very important role in the progress of the "action" and was one reason for the passivity of the Jewish masses.

The first of the privileged categories was made up of the employees of the *Judenrat,* policemen and hospital staffs; these were definite, closed groups that could not be expanded beyond their permanent ranks.

For this reason, people ran en masse to the German firms operating in the ghetto; people paid these firms fabulous sums to be listed among their workshop personnel and to obtain sometimes semifictive documents.

In addition, various workshops were set up by the Jews. The rush took on an epidemic, tragicomic character; in premises that only yesterday housed cafés or restaurants, the decor was hastily switched: machines were installed that were supposed to produce who knows what objects. Many Jews enrolled in these shops, lists were submitted to some unknown official, people rushed in to them from all sides, often trying to fool even themselves. Unfortunately, this did not last long, and all these workshops that had sprung up like mushrooms soon became perfect targets for roundups.

I no longer remember if it was the interpretation of the first notice or some supplementary order, but the exemption from deportation was extended to the staffs of Mutual Aid. This was a fact of prime importance, because this category included a broad stratum of the population; it was not a closed group, but one that could be enlarged, which thus apparently allowed for the possibility of saving a large number of human lives. During the first days of the *Aktion*, my colleagues and I were totally immersed in this problem.

For the workers of Mutual Aid, a new sort of personal exemption papers was printed—green, if I'm not mistaken. For the first ten to twelve days of deportation, when the roundups were carried out only by the Jewish police, these papers were honored. They were issued by Wielikowski, in his role as head of social services of the *Judenrat* and president of the Official Aid Committee.

I remember that on the third or fourth day after the start of the deportations, I received a visit from Dr. Ringelblum, who told me of the *Judenrat*'s decision that exemption documents would be issued only to the paid employees of Mutual Aid and not to volunteer workers. Ringelblum was deeply agitated and indignant about this. As one of the creators and organizers of the Public Sector, he understood how unjust it was to refuse protection to a large number of self-sacrificing relief workers for the mere reason that they were not on the payroll of Mutual Aid. Ringelblum proposed that I go immediately to the meeting of representatives of political groups that was taking place right at that moment at 52 Leszno Street. This meeting had drawn a rather sizeable number of people. Among the participants, I recall noticing A. Landau, S. Sagan, and M. Kirszenbaum. We stated why we had come to the meeting. Our point of view met with general approval, and it was decided that we should have a discussion with Wielikowski. I was supported on this issue by, among others, my friend, the lawyer Mieczyslaw Warm, legal advisor to the Official Aid Committee who, happily, escaped the catastrophe.

At the end of the discussion, the question was reviewed and the right to obtain exemption papers from Mutual Aid was extended to the workers in the Public Sector. As far as I can remember, this right was granted only to the relief workers of the Center and the Districts, thereby excluding members of Housing Committees, but as it was Mutual Aid that decided on the validation of papers, this still allowed us considerable possibilities for saving broader segments of the population.

Clearly it was impossible for us not to foresee the following dilemma: If the number of exemption papers is limited, as in other groups, they may be able to guarantee, at least for a certain period of time, the safety of their bearers; on the other hand, if they are given out to more people, they will inevitably lose, by force of circumstances, all their efficacy. Nevertheless, from the very first, even without discussions on this subject, the Public Sector set about procuring exemption papers for everyone who had participated to any degree in its work. Eventually, of course, the number of requests, and outright pleas, for papers rose steadily. In order to discuss the situation thus created, we called together a meeting one night (meetings held by day were ceaselessly interrupted by the raids) in the offices of the sixth district, at 29 Nowolipki Street. Seated at the table were the board representatives of Mutual Aid, the Public Sector, and part of the office of the Central Commission of Tenement Committees, with a certain number of relief workers also in attendance. We were accompanied by our families, who were afraid to stay at home, for the roundups often began at dawn. It would be hard to forget this night meeting of ghosts: The office didn't have enough furniture in it for all the participants, and those worn-out people sat scattered over the whole room, leaning against the walls. Although we were taken up with our work, we still took turns sleeping for a half hour in some corner; but basically we held our assembly all night without interruption. In the course of this meeting, we prepared Mutual Aid exemption papers for a great many people. This did indeed create inflation, and two or three days later the Jewish police stopped honoring them. By the time of the next roundups, in which the Germans took part, documents from Mutual Aid had lost all their efficacy.

The *Aktion* meanwhile continued without letup, and every day inexorably claimed thousands of victims. Human words are impotent to describe how all these people went to their deaths and how those who still awaited theirs lived from hour to hour, moment to moment.

For one day or another—inevitably—they would be taken in a raid that would be fatal to them.

The roundups were becoming routine for us. The Jewish police would close in on a house, and you would hear the order: "Everyone into the courtyard—and keep the apartment doors open!" Next, a thorough search of lodgings would begin; those who were hiding were dragged into the courtyard (later, the Germans would simply kill them on the spot); this would be followed by a document check, and the victims would be led off.

Once—this was around ten days after the start of the *Aktion*—our house was surrounded while I was away. By then, having papers from Mutual Aid meant very little. My wife told to me that she had twice tried to hide; she was discovered by a Jewish policeman, who dragged her into the courtyard; even so she made a third attempt and managed to escape; otherwise, she would never have made it back alive.

On another occasion I was present when a roundup was taking place in our building. It was led by an officer of the

Jewish police, the lawyer L. (who later died in the camp at Poniatow). He was wearing high yellow boots and an elegant tunic, and he held a riding crop in his hand: in every aspect of his appearance he was trying to imitate an SS man. He led off twenty people from our apartment house; the apartment next to ours, where the family of a jeweler was living, was completely emptied of its inhabitants. And while we still heard the sound of their footsteps in the street, some of the police agents burst into the apartment and set about looking for jewels they were convinced were hidden about the rooms.

Each raid threw everyone into confusion and anxiety for a few minutes; then the small cares of daily life took over again. People would rush all around to find some scrap of nourishment, now harder than ever to come by; women would light the fire in the kitchen, do the wash, scrub their children . . . . This would not last very long—just until the next order of "Everyone into the courtyard!"

And there was something infinitely agonizing and appalling in this tangle of nightmare and ordinary life.

In this period, any limit between life and death had disappeared in the ghetto, the slip out of life into death had lost its gradual character, was now a plunge into the void . . . . Death permeated life with an imperious obviousness, yet it all seemed so farfetched, so unexpected.

A family that, just a few moments earlier, was sitting peacefully at table, disappeared suddenly, as though conjured away by some evil spell. I know of many cases where a man who had gone out for a short time, on coming home, found neither his wife, nor his children, nor his aged parents. The man came home: Everything was in its place in his apartment—the table with the leavings of an interrupted meal, the notebook in which his child was learning to write its first letters, toys . . . . Only the human beings who animated these poignant, henceforth useless objects, did not answer to any call—having ceased to exist.

This invasion of death that swept aside every trace of human life appeared so contrary to nature that whatever happened now lost its reality, seemed a macabre fantasy or the effect of black magic. This is why, in the depths of our consciousness there lingered the hope that some magic word would be found, that one would have only to make some gesture—and the nightmare would vanish, and everything would fall back into place. The grandiose absurdity of this annihilation that was taking place in the world kept its victims from realizing its inescapability. Often I would chance to speak to people who, only an hour before, had lost through a roundup the beings dearest to them. They would speak of them—this always struck me—without the despair, pain, or anguish they would have shown had the same thing happened in normal times. Instead, their behavior expressed a sort of resigned surprise, as they refused to understand what had happened, refused to believe that the universe in which they lived could fall prey to such unlikely delirium, could destroy so senselessly themselves and those closest to them. It seemed to them that this bad dream would lift at any moment, that it was simply necessary to find some way to survive while waiting to wake up. Thus the owners of shops moved with their families into their stores, boarding up the door and leaving only a small, narrow exit. They were under the illusion that in this way no one could find them and take them off.

A young woman I knew told me one day that she had hidden her elderly parents in the ruins of a house destroyed by bombings; every evening, when the raids had finished, she brought them some food. She thought they could hold out in this fashion until the moment when all this would be over, since it was only a matter of time before this horror would cease.

When the number of scheduled victims for the day was reached, the *Aktion* stopped, to recommence the following dawn. We would be told of the end of the day's *Aktion* by the Jewish police as they returned from it. They also informed us at what hour it was slated for the following day. Up to that hour, the danger was removed. The ghetto looked then like a crushed antheap: people would leave their holes, walk into other streets to see how things were at their relatives' and friends' houses. And only too often did it happen that, in cases like these, I would find an apartment empty, its doors ajar.

As time went on and the raids were carried out by the Germans in ever more brutal fashion, not only apartments, but whole tenement buildings and streets were emptied out.

I recall, toward the end of August, going down ghostly Pavia Street—once so populous, and now without a trace of human life. The doors to empty apartments were wide open: no one was left there to be further plundered . . . .

The human prey captured in the roundups were usually lined up and led on foot toward the deportation center. Yet sometimes, the victims were crammed into the omnibuses of the firm Kohn & Heller or loaded onto open horse-drawn carts. I can still see those heavily loaded carts. Most of the people accepted their fate meekly, passively, some made farewell signs to relatives who had not been captured in the raid and stood off at a safe distance; a few held up their papers to the police, trying to convince them they should not be deported or pleading with them to be released. But the policemen paid no heed to the people loaded onto the carts: their only concern was to take the prescribed number of victims back to the *Umschlagplatz*. Once I saw on Nowolipki Street, a woman of about thirty-five who was trying to jump from the car and was shouting hysterically to the policeman: "Let me go, I'm a schoolteacher, do you understand—a schoolteacher." But the agent who pushed her back into the car answered her: "The Germans don't need a schoolteacher, they need laborers."

The terrible fratricidal role the Jewish police had to fulfill in the extermination of the Warsaw ghetto was only the logical culmination of the path it had followed ever since its creation, and what made it so hateful to most of the Jews.

Yet all the same, the institution of a Jewish ghetto police ought to have been considered, under these conditions, a fortunate solution; for clearly a community of more than 400,000 souls could not do without them, and it was better for this function to be entrusted to the Jews rather than remaining in the hands of the Germans or the so-called "blue" Polish police loyal to them. It seemed, similarly, that by virtue of its makeup, it would have to carry out its mission honorably: many intellectuals—lawyers, engineers, etc.— joined it, and undoubtedly they had good intentions. But at the same time it contained dubious elements, put into it at the instigation of the Germans, or under the protection of members of the *Judenrat*. And, not long after its creation, it became altogether clear that the darker elements in it had gained the upper hand, and that the entire police force had been transformed not only into a deeply corrupt organization, but a mob of gangsters.

This cannot be said, obviously, of all its members. There were, admittedly, men in it who maintained their integrity and suffered from not being able to quit the ranks; for resignations were not accepted, and those who wished to withdraw from duty were threatened with reprisals from the Germans. I recall, for example, a young colleague of mine in Mutual Aid, the engineer Kleinerman, who had left us as soon as the ghetto was created to join the police force. I had lost sight of him, but then about a year later, in the winter of 1942, I spotted him at the street post they'd given him as an ordinary patrolman. I was startled to see him in this role, because his education qualified him for a higher position. We began chatting. He told me that at the outset he had worked in the office, but so many abominable things happened there, that, because he was not allowed to resign, he had chosen to become a patrolman—his only chance to keep any distance from them. Kleinerman was clearly not alone in this, though the fact doesn't change the criminal and antisocial nature of the Jewish police.

Nevertheless, even by the time there was no longer any doubt about its nature, a certain number of young intellectuals tried to join the police. This can be explained, in the first place, by the hope of averting danger for themselves and their families; but another factor was sheer desire for power—a complex from which certain Polish Jewish groups, denied public functions, suffered. Thus, an irreproachable colleague from Mutual Aid, the lawyer T., asked me one day if he would be struck from the ranks of our members in the event he joined the police, who were tempting him with the chance to direct legal services for them. I answered him that we made no provision for removal from office, but I tried to discourage him from taking this step. I think he followed my reasoning, and it was only at the start of the *Große Aktion* that I glimpsed him on the street wearing a policeman's cap.

I shall not dwell on the corruption that reigned in police circles, and had it not consisted of taking bribes from speculators, it might have found certain justifications.

For a prolonged period the Jewish police were unpaid, but, for compensation, they took contributions from residents: the Tenement Committees would receive orders to donate a certain sum before an appointed date. In the event of non-payment, the building was put under blockade: the doors were closed, and the tenants could not set foot on the street. One day, this occurred in the building in which I was living. Intending to go to a meeting, I tried to get out. Near the door I saw two agents commanded by a police officer, the lawyer Sz., with whom I had only recently defended someone in a trial. We looked at each other without a greeting, and he motioned to his agents to open the door.

The Jewish police wanted at all costs to imitate the "true public powers": a complicated hierarchy was set up, with a spectacularly fastidious respect for rank. This attitude was often grotesque, but in the overall scheme of things, it was an utterly insignificant fact, hardly worth discussing at length.

I recall the following episode: In November of 1941, some friends and I entered a café on Siena Street. We had various matters to discuss, and there was a little room off to the side, where we could talk in peace. Peering into the large room, we noticed a large table lavishly spread, around which were seated some forty Jewish and Polish policemen, who seemed to be in a very jolly, lively mood. We discovered that this was a celebration on the occasion of the first anniversary of the two forces' collaboration. We also found out that this was merely the continuation of the celebration, which had begun with a dinner in the restaurant Sztuka and had cost an enormous amount. It was paid for by its hosts—the Jewish police.

The Jewish police often lent a helping hand to gangsters: the police would burst in at night on tenement buildings and terrorize the Tenement Committees, demanding that young people be handed over for them to carry out jobs. In most cases these jobs were invented by the police: having obtained a ransom payment, they withdrew. Sometimes they would organize roundups on the streets and free the people arrested, again for a ransom.

During the *Große Aktion* the Jewish police, having discovered the hiding places where women and children had taken refuge, turned them over to the Germans. I recall that whenever a policeman was seen on the grounds of the Landau brothers' carpentry shop, he inspired the same fear that a German would have. After the end of the war, someone told me at the Polish Ministry of Justice that an officer in the Jewish police, the lawyer S., had been arrested for having revealed the location of shelters where Jews had hidden.

Clearly, I have given only a cursory presentation of the infamous role the Jewish police played; but I consider that, after having told of the worthy and self-sacrificing conduct of most Jews under the inhuman conditions of ghetto life, it was my duty also to mention its baser elements.

XV. THE LIFE OF A JEWISH WORKSHOP AT THE TIME OF THE *GROßE AKTION*—THE ESCAPE OF THE AUTHOR'S WIFE

At the beginning of August, after the protection papers of Mutual Aid had lost any value, our situation—mine and my wife's—got so dangerous that we were threatened with deportation at the next roundup. It was at this point that my friend and colleague, Alexander Landau, offered to settle us in the factory he and his brother Jozef owned. This shop was part of the network of German workshops, was supervised by a German police chief, and seemed to offer, at least temporarily, a certain safety.

Throughout my narrative I have had occasion to mention this small shop, which had become a haven for community relief workers. When I arrived, in fact, I found there several colleagues from Mutual Aid. In addition, though, people from quite varied social circumstances begged the Landau brothers to be let in there. They were rarely refused, and the premises became jam-packed. There were people from all walks of life, of all ages, and many were women—and not one had the least notion of how a carpentry shop operated. It was impossible to legalize the situation of such a multitude, but the Landau brothers did all in their power to save everyone. By working out an arrangement with the German police chief (his name was Gans) they managed to do so, up until a certain point.

The contribution of this workshop to the potential of the German war effort was not very significant: it made cupboards for officer's barracks; but for the entire length of my stay, there were no more than two or three shipments. The machines were idle most of the time. But as soon as the signal was given that the Germans were approaching, the motors were turned on, and you heard the futile buzz of machines running in neutral. For us this noise was an alarm signal. Some of the "workers" took shelter in previously prepared hiding places; others took their places behind the work benches and pretended to be diligently occupied. But soon all these subterfuges lost their effect. The Germans began conducting the raids themselves brutally, ruthlessly; the Jewish police only stood by and carried out secondary functions. Yet all that would come only later; during the first phase of our stay in the carpentry shop—while the Germans finished liquidating the ghetto as a city—we were relatively safe there.

Living conditions in the little factory were rough. We were in very cramped quarters, lacking the most basic conveniences. The property didn't even have running water. The precariousness of sanitary conditions gave most of the inhabitants dysentery, often accompanied by fever. A moral and physical lassitude and apathy took hold of us. We were never alone, always surrounded by a crowd; at night we could not undress. Our moral equilibrium was shattered. Among us were many who had lost their nearest kin in the previous roundups, while others were forever worrying about their fate. The national catastrophe occurring before our very eyes plunged us into a deep depression.

And despite everything—such is our inexhaustible instinct for self-preservation—this makeshift, anxious society had started to crystallize into bizarre yet definite forms.

It seems impossible for me to convey any adequate sense of this life to those who did not themselves experience it; but let me at least note a few of its aspects.

A police force was established to guard the factory and see that discipline was maintained inside. Likewise, a judge's bench was called for, and I, in fact, was assigned to it. The police force handled pretrial investigations and drew up reports that it entrusted to me for judgment.

Of all the institutions I have ever belonged to in all my judicial work in Russia and Poland, this court was surely the most original. The cases were fairly numerous, for conflicts often arose among the inhabitants and violations of the norms of cohabitation and factory regulations were not uncommon. Thus, our tribunal judged civil and criminal cases, relying on a brief procedure that I devised and the workshop board authorized. Among our sanctions, the maximum sentence was expulsion from the factory—the equivalent of a death sentence. Obviously, this sentence was never carried out, and in the vast majority of cases we were confined to issuing reprimands and warnings for the future. Compromises were often worked out between litigants.

Here, for example, is a case of civil law that quickly comes to mind: The plaintiff demanded restitution of a diamond he had entrusted to the defendant. The latter, to explain the diamond's disappearance, claimed he had entrusted it to an intermediary who had been deported.

On the face of it, the court session was rather idyllic: I presided with the two assessors I required in a small side courtyard, under the shade of an old tree. As time went on, our sessions were more and more frequently interrupted by roundups, in which event the judges, plaintiffs, and the accused would march off together into the ranks of the victims destined to fill the deportation quotas.

The Landau brothers did all they could to make food available. Thus, the small factory owned some cows, whose milk was divided between children and the sick; at the end of August these cows were requisitioned by the Germans. The plant had a bakery of its own. It also had an official food-supply warehouse. But, since the Germans provided food only for the recorded number of workers, which was minimal compared to the actual number of people in hiding there, the food supply was inadequate. The main way to procure food was through individual purchases of goods smuggled into the ghetto. The black market functioned even in this period, but prices never stopped rising; and I remember that we had to pay one hundred zlotys for a kilo of bread, at the time an astronomical sum.

The contraband reached the ghetto by way of the Jewish cemetery, not far from the carpentry shop. For quite a while now—ever since 1941, I think—the Jewish cemetery officially lay beyond the ghetto's borders. Only the dead and the morticians' staffs could enter it; even the immediate families of the deceased, if they wanted to attend the funeral, had to obtain special authorization. The cemetery was the site, then, at which food was purchased from smugglers from the Aryan side. The morticians' staffs had the supplies brought into the ghetto in hearses once they were emptied of their burdens, the dead, who had often succumbed to typhus or other illnesses. But famine kept us from dwelling on the unhygienic nature of our food supplies.

After a roundup, or at other moments of calm, the women left the grounds of the factory to try to find some food in the neighborhood. One day, someone passed the word that not far from our workshop there was meat for sale. My wife went out with the others, but shortly after she left, a huge roundup began that included our little factory and the neighboring properties. When the raid was over, my wife had still not returned. It was more than likely that this time she had become a victim. Finally, about an hour after the raid had ended, someone informed me that my wife was in the infirmary. I rushed there and could see, as I arrived, that someone was bandaging her feet, which were covered in blood. Here is her own account of what happened that day, and the adventures of the following days:

Not far from the factory, I saw the spot where the meat-seller had set up; I joined the line with the others but then, moments later, someone shouted a warning to us that the Germans were on their way. In a flash the crowd scattered. Since I did not have enough time to make it back to the carpentry shop, I dashed to the opposite side and wound up in a deserted courtyard; everyone who had been in it had hidden. At one side of this enclosure I noticed a piece of sheet metal which was leaning against a girder, forming a narrow shelter between itself and the ground. With not a second to lose, I took refuge under this sheet metal strip. It was totally silent around me, but all of a sudden, a few steps away from my hiding place, a German appeared, pointing his gun ahead of him. He had scaled a pile of boards and was carefully surveying the courtyard. The strip of sheet metal concealing me was small, and it would be hard for me not to be discovered. Knowing that anyone found hiding was shot point-blank, I wait-ed, with my heart pounding, for a shot to come flying in my direction. I was afraid that no one would find me and that I would vanish without a trace. So I put my passport in my hand, ready to fling it from me at the last moment into the courtyard, in the hope that later someone would find it and take it back to our factory. It is hard for me to tell how much time passed, but I heard the abrupt cracking of boards collapsing under the weight of the German; he nearly fell and soon left the lot. Moments went by and people emerged in the courtyard: The roundup was over. I called for help and they extricated me from my hiding place, surprised that I had managed to work my way into such a tight space. I returned to the factory, my feet covered with wounds. They greeted me there with amazement: I had been given up for lost.

I do not know if this was pure chance or a series of miracles, but in reflecting on my life under German occupation, I must admit that I often found myself in seemingly hopeless situations. Death seemed inevitable, yet, always at the last instant, something unexpected happened that saved my life.

A few days before the episode I've just recounted, the Germans had captured around 300 women and children in our little factory. It was a fine, sunny day and, because of the stifling heat in our overcrowded carpentry shop, the management had advised the women to go and let their children out in a nearby clearing where there was a bit of grass and some trees. No one made it back from there: the Germans lined them all up and led them straight off to the *Umschlagplatz*. By a pure fluke, I had not followed the other women and remained on the factory grounds. This time I was saved, but it was obvious that the situation of the women in the factory was desperate: one day or another, they would be deported.

Despite this hopeless situation, neither my husband nor I had yet envisaged the possibility of fleeing into the Aryan city. We were so shaken by the general extermination that the idea of escaping individually did not occur to us. In the factory, we were very friendly with a young couple, the engineer Perelrot and his wife Lucy. She was a very pretty woman, with lots of energy and initiative. She began trying to persuade me to go with her into the Aryan city so that, once we had found our own way there, we could get our husbands out too. She had a sister there who would help us find Aryan papers.

My husband managed to get through by telephone to his old friend, the lawyer Zygmunt Wolosewicz, who had promised, despite the risk he would be taking, to shelter us, at least for some time, in his apartment.

The day for the escape came. I put on several dresses and a coat (in order to have spare clothes for later on), sewed money into my belt, and joined Lucy Perelrot in the lines of the workers who were being sent every morning to the Jewish cemetery to tend the vegetables that had been planted in unoccupied areas.

At the entrance to the cemetery there were German inspectors; the sentinels were making a superficial search of the people reporting for work there. We managed to pass through their inspection without a hitch and reached the cemetery. Alexander Landau had assigned the head of the commando unit to find us a "ferryman," that is, a smuggler, to get us across, but the man in question refused to deal with us, and we were forced to look for one ourselves. At the cemetery there were many people drifting around, waiting to smuggle in food supplies. One of them, who looked like a real ruffian, agreed, for a certain sum, to show us an appropriate spot to climb over the cemetery wall.

Just at this moment we saw Germans in front of us. This time we were not going to be lucky: it was the first roundup ever to take place in the cemetery. My first thought was to hide somewhere, but it was too late—I had to join the line. The Jewish police were participating in this raid: among the policemen, I could see the lawyer B., whom I knew well; I spoke to him, but he replied that he had no power to do anything for us.

Our march toward the *Umschlagplatz* was about to begin, when the situation changed: the German police chief for our factory, Gans, appeared in the cemetery. He had come especially to defend our unit, which was under his command—and he succeeded in his task. We were saved, but for how much longer?

Before my very eyes, the Germans killed a poor woman who had not put the prescribed Jewish armband on her sleeve; her two children clung, sobbing, to the corpse of their mother.

Our ferryman, who had vanished as soon as the Germans approached, reappeared. He led us toward the cemetery wall and told us to jump over it one at a time. He chose to take care of my friend first and went off with her, telling me to wait in the same spot. Twenty minutes went by that seemed an eternity. I was in a panic that our smuggler would not come back and that I would thus be obliged to stay all alone in the cemetery, since our commando unit had already left; before me, strewn over the ground, torn into little pieces, were my Jewish papers. Just then, the ferryman returned; he helped me scale the wall from inside, but then told me to jump and to shift for myself, alone, because he was afraid that as a pair we would be spotted by the German police.

I had no choice: I jumped. After that, everything went splendidly; no one in the street paid any attention to me, and I was able to go freely on my way.

A strange feeling came over me at the sight of a normal street, where passersby were walking calmly along and where a trolley car was circling on its route. I could board that trolley and go directly to Mr. Wolosewicz, but if I had I would have lost sight of my friend. Out of prudence, we had not told each other our addresses, and agreed to meet up in a nearby apartment building where my friend knew the concierge and would be waiting for me. I went to this address. But on entering the courtyard, I was horrified to see my friend, pale and dishevelled, flanked by two women. It was clear to me that she had fallen into the clutches of informers who were blackmailing her. We pretended not to know each other, but the expert eye of these villainous women spied me out as another defenseless victim. They threw themselves on me, pulled me into a dark corner and demanded money and jewelry, frisking me in the coarsest way. They stripped me thoroughly, even removing my underwear, and left me only my dress. Luckily, they had not noticed the tight belt into which I had sewn my money. That was another miracle: without money it would have been impossible for me to pay for Aryan papers. Unsatisfied with their meager booty, but obviously assuming they had nothing more to gain from me, these two harpies finally let me leave. I stepped out of the courtyard; having no more strength to walk, I hailed a cab. But no sooner had the hackney had time to start moving than the two cutthroats reappeared. I was desperate. Not knowing what to do, I leapt from the cab and started running; the two harpies and the cab pursued me. At the corner of the street, I dashed into the first courtyard I found, made my way into the concierge's, and started asking after some imaginary tenant, at the risk that by my very desperate air, he would be able to guess who I was. At this moment, the door opened and the cabdriver entered. I tried to hide from him behind an armchair, but he forced me to leave, and told me that those two terrible women had left and he would take me where I wanted. I collapsed in the cab and our ride began. But I had not yet come to the end of my ordeals: the coachman informed me that he understood very well that I was a Jew; he insisted I show him my papers and threatened me, demanding money. After long bargaining, we settled on a certain sum I was to pay him on my arrival. Not wishing to reveal the address of our friend the lawyer, I gave him the address of a girlfriend of mine, the dressmaker S.R. She was a generous woman, and a true daredevil, who did her utmost to help everyone she could. We stopped before the house, the cabbie stepped down from his seat with the intention of following me, but I managed to escape him and he could not see what apartment I was entering. The first person I saw there was a Jewish woman lawyer, S.L., who lived in the same building as we did, but who had escaped from the ghetto a little earlier. She gave me the amount I needed to pay my driver. After resting up a bit, I went to see a cousin of mine who lived in the neighborhood. She had never accepted the reality of the ghetto and simply stayed on in Warsaw, availing herself of an Aryan I.D. I spent three days at her house; she could not keep me there longer, since she herself lived in perpetual terror. I then went to find our friend the lawyer, who practically greeted me with the question: "Do you know what's waiting for you over here?" he asked me. I didn't answer him, and he gave the answer himself: "Death." I said to him: "I have no choice: It's death here or death there." So began my "Aryan" life. I had the feeling of being a hunted animal. Every day I phoned my husband at the factory. At an appointed hour, he would wait by the telephone for my call. I told him of my desire to return to the factory, but he was categorically opposed to the idea. Then one day I called, and someone who answered from the factory informed me that my husband was no longer there, that he had been taken that very day by the Germans . . . .

XVI. LAST DAYS IN THE GHETTO
THE AUTHOR'S DEPORTATION AND ESCAPE

The morning our wives fled, the engineer Perelrot and I observed the events going on in the cemetery from our factory. Once we saw the Germans enter, we realized the danger our work unit was in; later we learned that, thanks to the intercession of engineer Landau, the German police chief had gone there to help them out. On his return, we heard that his mission had been crowned with success; a while later the entire commando crew came back, with the exception of our wives. Thus they had managed to get away, and, posted near the telephone, we impatiently awaited their news.

As our factory was under German management, it had a telephone, and two lines at that. We would use one to telephone into the city, while the other was to remain free for incoming calls. This way we were able to communicate, at least by telephone, with the outside world. But finally, for whatever reasons, if not quite simply by mistake, one of our lines was taken off the phone network; so we were left with a single line, which was a source of torment for us. Hundreds of people living in the plant wanted, for various reasons, to communicate with the Aryan city: to be informed of the fate of close kin who were in hiding, to make contact with Polish friends to prepare for an escape, to give Poles authorization for their possessions, etc. A quantity of people were always standing around the telephone, waiting their turn and nervously fighting over the receiver. Given these conditions, the line was always busy and the factory officials necessarily forbade this. But the prohibitions accomplished nothing, and it was almost impossible to telephone from the city to the carpentry shop. Nonetheless, many continued to wait for news from outside concerning issues as vital as those that prompted our calls from the factory. The chance of receiving the awaited phone communication seemed a matter of life and death, bringing perhaps some hope of rescue. Those awaiting phone calls would beg the others not to tie up the line the whole time and to give them the chance to receive calls. But the people wanting to telephone were equally pressed, and their situation equally hopeless . . . . Scenes of despair, fits, and nervous panics, went on by the telephone morning, noon, and night.

Between August 20 and 25, the ghetto had definitely lost the look of a homogeneous urban area, and was transformed into so many islets, each occupied by a mill or workshop. The tenements that had been emptied of their inhabitants were made available now to the workshops, for housing their personnel; our factory received a block of apartments on Mila Street. Engineer Perelrot, two employees of the factory—a mathematician with a degree from Oxford and a dentist, both of whose names I have forgotten—and I were able to take a two-room apartment.

In the area where our block of tenements ended, the street was barricaded by a fence, behind which were posted guards who all came from eastern countries: Ukrainians, Latvians, etc. The heat was unbearable that summer; sometimes in the evenings people would go out in front of the entrances to their buildings. It was not rare to see these guards, for the sheer sport of it, shoot in our direction, at times with fatal results.

We would walk to and from the factory in close ranks; by this time anyone who set foot on the street alone was at once taken off to the *Umschlagplatz*. In the daytime, during work hours, inspections were often carried out in the apartments; anyone found there would be taken off for deportation. For this reason, even a sick person with a temperature of 104°F was obliged to go to the factory every day.

One evening, on returning home, we found a woman who had ventured into our apartment, from where, I don't know. She was twenty-five, pretty, and under normal circumstances men would have eagerly sought her company. But now, she felt she was a burden to herself and others; since she was not registered in the factory, she had no right to live in our apartment and was forced to remain hidden in the building all day, especially when inspections were most frequent. She stayed with us for about a week; one evening when we came back from the factory, we no longer found her there. We did learn, however, that no inspection had taken place that day. She must have left of her own free will, having found another hiding place that seemed less risky.

The roundups at the factory continued, claiming increasing numbers of victims from our ranks. Rumors were circulating that they would spare the lives of men only up to the age of thirty-five. The older men tried to appear younger and dyed their gray hair. This operation was carried out by the factory's barber, but as his dye was of very poor quality, the men came out with highly unconvincing hair color; yellowish, reddish, greenish. The combination of these haggard faces with fantastically colored hair made a gloomy sight indeed, a sort of macabre masquerade.

Around August 25, we were all given the order to line up in front of the factory building to listen to an important speech by the German chief of police. In rather friendly fashion, he informed us that the *Aktion* in our factory was over; he guaranteed safety to all those who remained and asked us to go about our work calmly. It is fair to assume he believed what he was saying, but the calm his speech elicited lasted only two days; then a new wave of raids commenced. Usually, the Germans leading the roundup demanded that the factory managers turn over to them a specific number of people to lead from our workshop to the *Umschlagplatz*. Apparently the Landau brothers had not accepted these terms: we were lined up, and the Germans themselves, as they saw fit, selected the day's victims. At the time of the roundup of September 4, Alexander Landau gave a sign to some people, myself among them, not to go out into the courtyard, but to stay in the office. We obeyed him and plunged into files, pretending to be diligently at work. The office was located on the ground floor, by an inner courtyard; the day was stifling, and the window wide open. We were seated, bending over our files, trying to make the least possible noise. All of a sudden a woman with disheveled hair, obviously quite out of control, jumped through the window into the room, shouting hysterically: "Hide me, I want to live too." And she quickly slid under the table where we were sitting. A moment later, the Jewish policeman from whom this woman was trying to escape entered the room. I can see him before my eyes as though it were happening today: He was a young man, oval-faced, with delicate features; he wore a pince-nez and was undoubtedly an intellectual. He ordered the woman to come with him and threatened that, if she did not, he would call in the Germans, which would mean death for all of us. Finally, he agreed to release the woman for a ransom of fifteen hundred zlotys. We promised to pay him this amount when the roundup was over, but he demanded the money on the spot, making it clear to us that he considered our lives too tenuous to be able to count on promises. We handed over the money we had with us and he took off.

But apparently the noise this scene provoked had drawn the attention of a nearby German. He burst into the office and shouted: *"Alle raus!"* (Everyone out!). We were forced to go into the courtyard and to join the people lined up there. A portion of them was already chosen for deportation, but the number of victims must have been too low. Two Germans, including the one who had herded us into the courtyard, continued the selection. When my turn came, the German said: "This one was hiding in the office," and pointed to me with a gesture that meant I should be deported. Thus I found myself among a rather important group of people flanked by the Jewish police; minutes later, we were lined up and our march toward the *Umschlagplatz* began. On the way, groups of people chosen from other factories joined us; by the time we approached the *Umschlagplatz* we formed a long line.

On our arrival, I noticed, seated on a tall chair, one of the major criminals in the Jewish police, Szmerling, surrounded by many policemen. The entrance to the square was here, formed by fences on both sides of the street; this passage, broader at first, progressively narrowed. We were led to enter behind this enclosure and made our way, pushed by those behind us, onto the *Umschlagplatz*. It was my first time there and I stayed only a short while. My impressions are therefore quite superficial. I can remember only a vast field that had, on one side, a large multistoried cement building and, in the center, rails where a long line of freight-train cars was standing; there were very few people in this field.

According to our information, several thousands of people were sometimes gathered onto the *Umschlagplatz*, filling every story of the large building; often the number of cars for the imminent departure of deportation candidates was too low, so that these people remained there several days. During this waiting period, it was not entirely impossible to be re-called and freed. On the march toward the *Umschlagplatz*, our small group of four people—the secretary general of Mutual Aid, Natan Asz, the lawyer Mirabel, the Jewish journalist Gutkowski, and myself—had decided to remain together, in the hope that a forceful intervention would be made on our behalf. Unfortunately, that day, there was no shortage of cars and they started loading us into them right away.

As soon as we found ourselves inside, the coffin lid closed over us: not even the Germans could remove anyone from the convoy. There was simply no precedent for that.

Sixty people were crammed into every freight car; we knew that on certain days they squeezed in more than a hundred, but the day of our deportation there was no lack of space. The cars were then sealed from the outside. The stifling heat was enough to suffocate us, air and light barely penetrated through a narrow opening in the wall. Despite the multitude of people, we still managed to sit, as best we could, on the floor. The train had not yet left, night was falling and the car interior was getting dark.

Suddenly the doors were opened, and the Ukrainian guards burst in shouting: "Give us your money," and started searching and plundering us. This occurred three times. Passively, without resistance, people turned over their money and personal effects. Eventually we started to be tortured by thirst. Women begged the guards: "Water! Give us a bit of water!" but they paid no attention.

The train rattled slowly, shunting over the Warsaw railway network, and starting and stopping several times. It was 8:30 P.M.. We heard an air-raid signal. The convoy stopped again. We were fervently wishing for a bomb to drop on our train, but heard only two or three distant detonations. A half hour later, the alert was over; the convoy started up again.

We were shaken as we first approached the *Umschlagplatz;* we refused to understand what was happening, tormented by a vague hope and by the terrible anxiety that this hope might not be fulfilled.

Yet once we were inside the freight car, a complete transformation came over us. I experienced an epic calm, my ideas grew clear, the only reality was the inevitability that awaited us. I viewed myself as an alien body, no longer a part of me. According to my observations, my comrades were experiencing something similar.

Our convoy crossed the Vistula, we could make out the Poniatowski Bridge, the trolley cars that circled on it, the beautiful city of Warsaw with all its splendors, a whole world where people could still breathe, live, love. While this picture unfolded before our eyes, we spoke of the fate that awaited us with terrifying objectivity. "Tomorrow," we said, "there will still be trolley cars and people wearing bright clothes on Poniatowski Bridge, but we won't exist any longer . . . ."

Only Asz, a young, very dynamic man, could not accept the idea of his vanishing. He was plunged in a gloom of despair and kept saying: "We've got to find a way to get out of this." I started to speak to him about an old book I admired very much, Boethius's *The Consolation of Philosophy*, but he

173

cut me off harshly: "What am I supposed to do with your philosophy at a time like this!"—"What value would philosophy have"—I answered—"if it didn't console at a moment like this?"

And the train kept on rolling through the night, toward the gas chambers of Treblinka.

I couldn't say at exactly what moment the idea came to us of trying to escape through the narrow opening in the wall. We had noticed that the strand of barbed wire sealing the car had come loose at several points. With the help of pocketknives we managed to remove it completely.

Gutkowski was the first to jump. Before he did, he had time enough to tell us that, a while before, he had finished writing a book on life in the ghetto. Usually he carried the manuscript with him, but some days before, he had given it to Giterman to read, and hoped in this way his manuscript would not get lost.

Our travel companions began to protest against our plan; they feared that once they arrived, they would be held responsible for us absentees. We replied that everyone had the right to act as he saw fit, and we urged them to follow our example.

But the truth is that for most of them this was physically unfeasible: the opening was too narrow and too high. They soon grew calmer.

The second one to jump was the lawyer Mirabel, the third—a young man whose name I didn't know. I turned to my neighbor, the dentist Segal, a community worker from the sixth district of Mutual Aid, urging him to follow, but he replied to me: "What's the use? They've taken my wife and my daughter. Either I'll find them alive again somewhere, or I'll die like them." The next man to jump was Asz.

The lawyer Mirabel was sick and very weak. After he had jumped, for as long as we could see him, he lay motionless on the ground. Later, we received no news of him; it is plausible, then, that he died immediately, on impact. Gutkowski and Asz were to die in the ghetto, to which they returned after their escape.

Now it was my turn. I didn't hesitate, although I had no confidence in the success of our undertaking; the night was very bright, and you could see almost as clearly as if it were day. If the guard were to catch sight of me from the window, he could shoot me right on the spot; yet I preferred to be shot rather than gassed. And what might I have to look forward to if my escape was successful? I recalled various cases of escape by political prisoners in czarist Russia. But at that time, once they crossed the border they were free and could at least lead lives worthy of human beings. Whereas I, I was condemned to live like a hunted animal, surrounded by hostile elements. The next two-and-a-half years would only corroborate my fears. My Aryan life proved harder and more painful than I could have imagined.

Several people hoisted me up to the opening, where I put in my feet, and they slowly pushed me out. Next I managed to grasp onto an overhang from the roof; thus I inched out by myself, dangling outside the freight car. Getting a look at the flat, sandy soil before me, I hurled myself forward and fell to the ground on my face—my ears were buzzing. Some time later, I lifted up my head. The convoy had vanished. I tried moving my hands and feet—they were intact. I felt my face and found my hands streaked with traces of blood and sand. I had wanted to take off my glasses before jumping but, at the last moment, I had forgotten to do so. They had broken, and left wounds on my face. Without losing any time I got up and hurried away from the railroad line. After walking for about ten minutes, I came to a pond. I washed my face, tore up my identification papers and threw them into the pond . . . . Michel Mazor ceased to exist . . . . An anonymous man now continued on his way. I came to a village (as I learned later, it was called Kobylka, and was three kilometers from the Zielonka station). It was four o'clock in the morning. I walked along a deserted street and came upon a peasant at work in his orchard. I asked him for shelter, which he refused quite gruffly, though he pointed to a pillared house nearby. The owner was gone; there was only a woman watching it. The peasant advised me to look for her, and I had no choice but to follow his advice. The gate was not shut, I entered the garden and sat down beneath a tree. It was about five o'clock in the morning. A woman came into the garden. I explained my situation openly to her. She led me into a barn, where I stretched out on the straw. She brought me coffee, tomatoes, and bread. I remained there until five o'clock in the afternoon. She could not let me stay there any longer, because another watchman, a rather untrustworthy man, would come to relieve her. She refused the money I offered her and took me out to the Warsaw road. The name of this generous-hearted woman was Sophia Migdalska. The house she was guarding belonged to Lieutenant Swiezawski. I intended to spend the night in the forest and set out for Warsaw in the morning, but soon a car drove by whose owner was headed for the city; he offered to take me along. A half hour before curfew, I found myself in the Warsaw suburb of Praga. The driver was going no further. Given the clothes I had on, I could not take the trolley car without attracting attention. So I set off walking very quickly, almost running, in the direction of the Vistula

Bridge. I had a long way ahead of me, however, and was not going to make it there in a half hour. Luckily I chanced upon a "rickshaw" that took me, for forty zlotys, to Zuravia Street. At 10 P.M., there I was sitting at table in the home of my old friend, the lawyer Wolosewicz. The next next day he went to tell my wife, who was then living in a sublet room, under the name of "Ms. Marie-Rosalie Mazurkiewicz." As he did not find her at home, he left her a note asking her to come at once to the house. A while later, looking out the window, I saw my wife coming up to the house. She rang, and it was I, whom she had given up for dead, who opened the door for her . . . . Three weeks later, I transformed myself into a native of the region of Vilna, Michael Maciejewski—and the most painful period of our trials began. It lasted until January 17, 1945. But that period no longer pertains to my memories of the ghetto. Perhaps I shall dedicate another chapter to it.

XVII. CONCLUSION

Several years have passed since the *Große Aktion* of the extermination of the Warsaw ghetto, a rather long period in human life, especially in an era as saturated in great events as ours. In this period we have seen the defeat of a Nazi beast that keeps trying to raise its head; we have been witness to the heroic struggle of the Jews of Palestine and the birth of the state of Israel; and we live in a world still atremble with premonitions of new storms brewing. It seems, then, that the events that unfolded in the ghetto—its life and its total destruction—may dim somewhat in our memory.

We all know how time, in its never-ending course, erases what the human soul has felt and experienced; the further the event has receded into the past, the more its vividness wanes; and one sees great sorrows and great joys gradually lose their emotional weight and sink into oblivion. It is precisely here that actuality passes into history.

If, from time to time, the subconscious allows the memory of a distant event to resurface, its emotional content is so weakened that it seems strange and unreal to the person who lived it.

This being the law of life, the reactions of the handful of Jews who survived the terrible years in Poland (and above all in Warsaw, the most grief-tried city on earth) are living proof against this law. For them, despite the progressive receding of events, the memories persist in all their tragic ineluctability, preserving the force and vividness of an eternal actuality.

The events of which we were both witnesses and victims were so extraordinary and incommensurable by any human standard that their occurrence is tantamount to a suspension of human history—which is why they remain stamped upon our souls in a permanent present.

Never before had humanity known such an epoch, when the brute forces born in its midst divided into two camps: hangmen and victims. The hangmen were the Germans, the victims—the Jews, primarily, but not just them. We must not forget the Russian prisoners of war, the elite of the Polish people, Serbian partisans, and countless others.

I do not intend here to solve the question of whether the German people in its entirety is responsible for Hitler's atrocities. One fact however remains indisputable: The bestial acts were perpetrated by segments of the population too broad to have been unknown to others, especially in the army. The Germans looked on these acts with an indifferent silence.

After the collapse of the Third Reich, they tried to justify this shameful attitude by a professed fear of the merciless cruelty the Nazi regime showed within the country, which forced everyone into silence. The least opposition roused, they claimed, reprisals so severe that only the heroes prepared to make vain sacrifices could summon courage to protest. But neither heroism nor voluntary martyrdom can be demanded of the masses.

Nonetheless, although terror incontestably reigned within Germany, too, it is false to assert that public opinion was altogether impotent there. We know, for example, that under pressure of general discontent, the regime was forced to yield to public opinion in the matter of euthanasia. The term is universally held to mean mercy killing, granting death out of compassion to someone afflicted with an incurable disease and the atrocious suffering that goes with it—its only motive being to shorten this useless suffering.

Among Hitler's followers, however, euthanasia meant something completely different: the mass extermination of people suffering from mental illnesses, weak constitutions, and, in general, the unproductive population.

Euthanasia was introduced in Germany the moment when war was declared. It was performed with the utmost secrecy, but reports of it reached the masses and stirred protests among ordinary citizens, the Church, certain members of the Nazi Party, and in some cases even the active resistance of the sick. Finally, although euthanasia was an essential part of Hitlerian eugenics, the regime had to abandon it under pressure of public opinion. On August 1, 1941, Hitler stopped enforcing euthanasia for Germans.*

Still more significant are the reactions that emerged in Germany after the war, when the possibility to justify oneself by one's impotence in the face of Hitler's terror was eliminated. Even after the fall of Hitler's regime, the overwhelming majority of Germans maintained an attitude of indifference to all its crimes.

It is not a matter here of isolated individuals nor of groups which, in the era of the Third Reich, were drawn into the Nazi sphere of influence; for they never learned and even now never regret anything. As the [Allied] occupation

---

* Cf. L. Poliakov: *Bréviaire de la Haine* [Harvest of Hate], Ed. Calman-Lévy, Paris, 1951, pp. 208-213.

regime relaxed its grip, these people started to form organized groups which not only glorified Nazism, but indulged in new excesses of anti-semitism, even to the extent of barbarously profaning Jewish cemeteries.

Nor is the issue that denazification was carried out by the German tribunals in superficial fashion and that the majority of trials ended in inadmissibly lenient judgments; for it is plausible that the judicial apparatus was not equipped to handle a social phenomenon of such huge dimensions.

What is much more significant is the reaction of the majority of the people, the attitude of the overall population. One might have assumed that once Hitler's yoke collapsed, the country would feel a basic indignation toward those who, by their acts, forever dishonored the very name of the German; that by a spontaneous impulse the people would cast all those men out of the national community. Nothing of the sort happened. On the contrary, the Nazis feel increasingly comfortable in Germany.

In the face of these phenomena, it is only natural for the human mind to boggle and to ask: What can explain all this unprecedented bestiality?

Yet the more one reflects on it, the more inconceivable the phenomenon appears. Indeed, the efforts to trace the origins of Hitlerism back to the essence of German culture are not altogether convincing. If one can find certain strains of it in Luther's savage anti-semitism, in Hegel's apotheosis of the Prussian state, in Fichte's ardent nationalism, and Nietzsche's *blonde Bestie,* it is on the other hand the German soul that gave birth to the mysticism of Jakob Boehme, the universalism of Leibniz and Goethe, the wisdom of Kant, the ethic of compassion of Schopenhauer, the enlightened humanism of Thomas Mann . . . .

At the same time it is absolutely false to consider Hitlerism as a more or less natural outcome of Germany's situation after the First World War. Neither this situation (nor any situation of any other country) could explain the horrific negative miracle that was Hitlerian Nazism.

It is true that Germany experienced a profound malaise after defeat, that its existence was undermined by inflation and unemployment; but can this explain the planned extermination of millions of defenseless human beings in crematorial furnaces? Could it give German women justification to rest their heads on pillows made from the hair of massacred Jewish women?

These two sets of events are utterly incommensurable; it is impossible to establish any relation between them. No psychological, historical, or sociological rationale can provide an explanation. All causal or final interpretation falls short. Isn't it preferable then to give up explaining this phenomenon? Any explanation, moreover, would contain an element of rationalization and, by that very fact, a certain apology for these unimaginable events; it would include them in the course of human history, whereas this ferocity, the explosion of these infernal forces, must remain outside the annals of all nations of the world . . . .

In the camp of the victims, the Jews were first; they had lost six million of their people. We have become so inured to that small statistical phrase, we repeat it so often that we have ceased to realize what it represents. But reflecting on it even a moment, one realizes a monstrous fact: six million martyrs! Lined up, their corpses could form a circle around the globe.

Most of them were obliged to go submissively to their deaths, and only a small number were able to die in a heroic struggle doomed from the start.

Jewish life has practically ceased in many countries; the largest Jewish community in Europe, that of Warsaw, disappeared completely.

Hundred of thousands of human beings were shut up in October of 1940 into the Warsaw ghetto and then hermetically cut off from any communication with the outside world. In this community, whose form was unprecedented in human history, hunger and exanthematic typhus raged from the start, and without letup, dispatching thousands to anonymous graves. The whole life of the ghetto was one ceaseless agony. In July 1942, the Germans started the systematic mass extermination of the ghetto's inhabitants: This action ended with the total destruction of the ghetto in May 1943. On May 16, 1943, the chief of police and of the SS in the Warsaw region, Jürgen Stroop, was able to announce triumphantly: "There is no longer a Jewish quarter in Warsaw."

All the occupants of the Warsaw ghetto were united by a common fate. They lived on a ship that was about to sink; in their closed-off world, one day was as uncertain as the next. And one is tempted to ask: What prevailed in the ghetto— the code of chivalry that obtains on a sinking ship, or the bestial instincts that stifle any human feeling of solidarity?

I have made no attempt to conceal the darker aspects of the ghetto; in addition to the abuses I have cited, there existed an Office for the Struggle Against Speculation, supported for a time by the Germans and, because it was based at 13 Leszno Street, called "the 13." This was an organization of gangsters and blackmailers, who even opposed the *Judenrat*. The mobile medic corps were similarly transformed into an instrument of terror, which, for a bribe, would spare the filthy apartments of the rich from disinfection, but scoured the dwellings of the poor so furiously that the few wretched goods they still had were often destroyed.

But corruption and demoralization never penetrated deeply into the general population. Most people showed tremendous tenacity and great resolve before the horrible sufferings to which they were exposed. Also, they created amazing, highly specific institutions of public relief. In extremely difficult conditions—under a ghetto administration that was indifferent and at times hostile—a great national movement was formed, based exclusively on the unpaid work of volunteers. This movement embraced the entire ghetto, with cells in all its housing (the Tenement Committees) steered by the Board of Directors of the Public Sector of Mutual Aid and by the Central Commission of Tenement Committees. It was the popular forces in the ghetto that bred and nurtured a heroic resistance against the Germans in the unforgettable days of April and May 1943.

No manifestation of ghetto life had a purely dark side: If one day Jewish policemen received an order to bring five victims each to the *Umschlagplatz,* and they carried this out, to save their own necks, with a zeal that did not even spare their own kin—on the other hand, there were cases, no less numerous, of people trying to take the place of their loved ones in the deportation lines and, when that was impossible, lining up with them: children alongside their parents, husbands alongside their wives . . . . Suffering purifies some people and debases others . . . . So it has always been.

But we must not forget that never before, in any human society, was the individual subjected to such trials as in the ghetto. Everyone was faced with the dilemma of either finding a scrap of bread by whatever means possible (and honest means were rare), or dying of hunger . . . . The questions of conscience posed to the inhabitants of the ghetto were many, painful, and unresolvable.

This is why, while paying homage to the martyrs and heroes of the ghetto, we must also grant some of its wrongdoers the chance to plead extenuating circumstances before the judgment of history.

INDEX OF NAMES